PRISON

HUMOR

Compiled by

Walter Allen

PRISON HUMOR
Copyright © 2010

ISBN-13: 978-1493683017

ISBN-10: 1493683012

Published by
Midnight Express Books

To my grandmother

The only one to be there for me.....

no matter what.

Ethel was a bit of a demon in her wheelchair and loved to charge around the nursing home, taking corners on one wheel and getting up to maximum speed in the long corridors. Because the woman was one sandwich short of a picnic, the other residents tolerated her and some of them actually joined in.

One day Ethel was speeding up one corridor when a door opened and Kooky Clarence stepped out with his arm out stretched.

"Stop!" he yelled in a firm voice. "Have you got a license for that thing?"

Ethel fished around in her handbag and pulled out a Kit Kat rapper and held it out to him.

"Ok." he said and away Ethel sped down the hall.

As she took the corner by the TV lounge on one wheel, Weird Harold Popped out in front of her and shouted "Stop! Have you got proof of insurance?"

Ethel dug around in her hand bag and pulled out a drink coaster and held it up to him.

Harold nodded and said, "On your way ma'am."

As Ethel neared the final corridor, Crazy Craig stepped out in front of her, butt-naked holding his you-know-what in his hand.

"Oh, good grief," yelled Ethel."Not that damn breathalyzer test again!"

A guy from Quebec and a guy from Ontario are fighting over a lantern when a genie pops out and grants each of them one wish.

The guy from Quebec says, "I want a wall around Quebec to protect my culture. Make it about 200 feet high, so nothing can get in or out."

"It is done," says the genie, turning to the other guy. "And your wish?"

The guy from Ontario smiles and says," Fill it with water."

A drunk stumbles out of a bar with a key in his hand.

A cop sees him and says, "Can I help you sir?"

"Yes, somebody stole my car."

The cop asks, "Where did you last see your car?"

"It was on the end of this key," says the man. The cop looks down and see's that the man's penis is hanging out of his pants.

"Sir, are you aware that you are exposing yourself?" the cop asks.

Confused, the drunk looks down and says, "My girlfriend is gone too!"

A man flops down next to a priest on the subway. The man's tie is stained, his face is smeared with red lip stick and a half empty bottle of rum is sticking out of his coat pocket. He opens a newspaper and starts to read.

After a few minutes, the guy turns to the priest and asks, "Say, Father, what causes arthritis?"

"Loose living, cheap, wicked women, too much alcohol and contempt for your fellow man."

"I'll be damned," the drunk says returning to his paper.

The priest, thinking about what he just said nudges the man and apologizes. "I'm very sorry. I didn't mean to be so harsh. How long have you had arthritis?"

"Oh, I don't have it, Father. It says here that the pope does."

A drunk walks into a bar, sits down, and demands a drink.

"Get out!" the bartender shouts. "I don't serve drunks here."

The guy stumbles out the front door, comes through the side door, sits down, bangs his fist and again loudly demands a drink.

"I thought I told you to get out," yells the bartender.

The drunk gets up, stumbles out the door and returns through the back door and angrily calls for a drink.

The bartender walks over and shouts, "I told you, no drunks aloud. Now get the hell out!"

The drunk looks up and slurs, "How many bars do you work at, anyway?"

A man dies and goes to hell. Satan asks, "Do you like to drink?"

"Sure," says the man.

"Well, you'll love Thursdays," says Satan. "All we do is drink beer, whiskey, vodka-everything. And you're dead, so no hangover!"

"Sweet," says the man.

"Do you like drugs?" asks Satan. "Because it's the same deal on Friday-all the drugs you can take!"

"Awesome!" says the man. "There has to be a catch to this."

"Not at all," says Satan. "You're gay, right?"

"No," says them man.

"Oh, well, then Saturdays are going to be a little rough!"

A biker walks into a yuppie bar and shouts, "All lawyers are assholes!" He looks around obviously hoping for a challenge.

Finally a guy comes up to him, taps him on the shoulder, and says, "Take that back!"

The biker says, "Why? Are you a lawyer?"

"No, I'm an asshole."

A union boss at a convention in Las Vegas decides to visit a local brothel.

He asks the madam, "Is this a union house?"

"No, I'm sorry, it isn't," she says.

"Well, if I pay $100.00, what do the girls get?" he asks.

"The house gets $80 and the girls get $20."

Mightily offended by such unfair dealings, the man stomps off in search of a more equitable shop.

Finally, he reaches a brothel where the madam says, "Why yes, this is a union house."

"And if I pay $100, what do the girls get?" he asks.

"The girls get $80 and the house gets $20."

"That's more like it!" the man says. He looks around the room and points to a gorgeous young redhead. "I'd like her for the night."

"I'm sure you would, sir, but..." says the madam, gesturing at a 70-year-old woman in the corner, "Ashley here has seniority."

A man walks into a bar with a shotgun in one hand and a bucket of manure in the other. "Give me a beer!" he demands.

"Sure thing," the bartender says.

The man drinks down one pint in one gulp, throws the bucket of manure into the air and blasts it with the shotgun. Then he walks out.

Four days later, the same man returns with his shotgun and another bucket of manure. He walks up to the bar and says, "Give me a beer."

"Wait, I remember you," the bartender says. "What the hell are you up to?"

"I'm training for a job as a state employee," the man says. "You know - drink beer, shoot the shit and disappear for a couple of days."

Two guys feel like a drink, but only have a buck between them so, one runs to the store and buys a hot dog.

"Follow my lead," he says as they go into a bar and order two shots. "When I stick the hot dog through my fly, get on your knees and start to suck it," he says. "We'll get kicked out."

His pal plays along, and sure enough, they get kicked out. They then use the trick at five more bars.

"I'm done," says the second guy. "My knees hurt and I'm starving."

"Not me," says the second guy. "I ate that hot dog three bars ago."

A man goes into a supermarket and buys a tube of toothpaste, a bottle of Coke, a bag of chips and a TV dinner. The cute girl at the register looks at him and says, "Single, huh?"

Sarcastically the guy sneers, "How'd you guess?"

She replies, "Because you're fucking ugly."

This guy sticks his head into a crowded barbershop and asks, "How long before I can get a haircut?"

The barber looks around the shop at all the customers and says, "About two hours," and the guy leaves.

Every day, the same guy pokes his head in at the busiest time and everyday he's told there's a long wait and he leaves.

Finally, after about two weeks of this, the barber looks over at a buddy and says, "Bill, why don't you follow that guy and see where he goes?"

In a little while, Bill comes back into the shop laughing hysterically.

"Well?" says the barber. "So, where does he go?"

"To your house."

A construction worker comes home just in time to find his wife in bed with another man. Incensed, he drags the man out to the garage and puts his Johnson in a vice. He secures it and removes the vice handle, then picks up a hacksaw.

The man, terrified, screams, "Stop! Stop! You're not going to...to cut it off are you?"

The husband shakes his head and hands him the hacksaw. "Nope, you are. I'm just going to set the garage on fire."

The cardinal was doing a crossword puzzle. He asked his assistant, "Can you think of a four letter word for a woman that ends in u-n-t?"

The assistant replied, "Aunt."

The cardinal said, "Of course, what was I thinking. Do you have an eraser?"

"I've been making a lot of Freudian slips lately," a guy says to his friend.

"Like what?" asks his buddy.

"Last week I asked the train conductor for two pickets to Tittsburgh."

"I did something similar the other day," says the friend. "My wife and I were having lunch and instead of saying, "Honey, pass the butter," I said "You fucking bitch, you ruined my life!"

One day when the teacher walked to the blackboard, she noticed someone had written the word 'penis' in tiny letters. She turned to the class, scanned the room looking for the guilty face. Finding not a guilty face in the room, she quickly erased the blackboard and begun her class.

The next day, the teacher went into the classroom and noticed, this time in larger letters, the word "penis" scrolled on the blackboard. Again, she looks around the classroom in vain for the culprit, but found none. And so, the teacher erased the blackboard and started the day's lesson.

Every morning for about a week, the teacher went into the classroom and found the same word on the blackboard; each day, scrolled bigger than the previous day.

Finally, one day, the teacher walked into the classroom expecting to be greeted by the same word on the blackboard. Instead, she found scrolled on the blackboard: "The more you rub it, the bigger it gets."

Q: What two words will clear out a men's locker room the quickest?

A: "Nice cock."

The navy decides to offer early retirement bonuses to its personnel. The rule is that a volunteer picks two spots on his body and gets $1,000 for every inch in between.

One officer asks to be measured from the top of his head to the tip of his toes; he's 6 feet tall and gets $72,000.

A second officer asks to be measured from the tip of his raised hand to his toes; he gets himself $95,000.

The third officer to volunteer is a mean old captain. "Measure me from the tip of my penis to my testicles," he demands.

The medical officer doing the measuring tells the captain this might not be terribly profitable. The captain insists and drops his trousers and the medical officer places the tape measure on the tip of his penis and starts to work his way back.

"My God!" the medical officer says in surprise. "Where are your testicles?"

The captain just smiles and says, "Vietnam."

Two horny collage freshmen are wandering around campus when they come across a dog licking his balls.

"Man, I wish I could do that," says the first student.

The second replied, "Don't you think you should pet him first?"

A lady walked into a car dealership and started to look around. Suddenly, she spotted the most beautiful car that she has ever seen and walked ever to check it out. As she bent forward to feel the fine leather upholstery, an unexpected little fart escaped. Embarrassed, she anxiously looked around to see if anyone had noticed and hoped a salesperson hadn't been nearby. But, as she turned back, there, standing next to her, was a salesman.

With a big smile he greeted her, "Good day, Ma'am. How may I help you today?"

Trying to maintain an air of sophistication and acting like nothing had happened, she smiled back and asked, "What is the price of this lovely car?"

Still smiling pleasantly, he replied, "Ma'am, I'm very sorry to say that I don't think I will be able to tell you the price."

Upset, the lady asks why he can't tell her the price and he responded by saying, "Ma'am, if you farted just touching the car then you are going to shit when you hear the price."

One morning in the office a man mentions to a coworker that her hair smells nice today. The woman suddenly grows enraged, storms into her boss's office and declares loudly that she's quitting and is going to file a sexual harassment lawsuit.

"Come on," says her supervisor. "What's wrong with a guy saying your hair smells nice?"

"He's a fucking midget!"

Two bored old ladies are sitting on a park bench. One says, "For five bucks, I'll streak through the flower show across the street."

They shake on it.

Waiting outside the flower show, her friend soon hears a commotion in the convention hall, followed by loud applause. Then, the naked granny burst through the door with a cheering crowd behind her.

"What happened?" asks her friend.

"I won first prize for best dried arrangement."

An old man is sitting on his porch one day when he sees a kid walk by with a roll of chicken wire under his arm. "What you gonna do with that chicken wire?" the old man asks.

"Gonna catch me some chickens," says the boy.

"You damn fool," the old man yells. "You can't catch chickens with chicken wire!"

But, that evening at sunset, the boy walks back dragging the chicken wire with about 30 chickens caught in it.

The next morning, the old man see's the boy walk by carrying a roll of duct tape. The old man yells out, "What you gonna do with that duct tape?"

"Gonna catch me some ducks," the boy yells back.

"You damn fool," the old man laughs. "You can't catch ducks with duct tape!"

But that night, the boy comes home trailing the unrolled roll of duct tape with about 35 ducks caught in it.

The next morning the boy walks by carrying a long reed. The old man asks, "Hey boy, whatcha got there?"

"It's a pussy willow," the boy answers.

"Wait up," the old man says, "I'll get my hat."

"I'm a Yankees fan," a first grade teacher explains to her class. "Who else likes the Yankees?" Everyone in the class raises their hand except one little girl. "Jamie," the teacher says surprised. "Why didn't you raise your hand?"

"I'm not a Yankees fan."

"Well, if you're not a Yankees fan, then what team do you like?"

"The Red Sox," Jamie answers.

"Why in the world are you a Red Sox fan?"

"Because my mom and dad are Red Sox fans."

"That's no reason to be a Red Sox fan," the teacher replies. "You don't always have to be just like your mom and dad. What if your mom and dad where morons? What would you be then?"

"A Yankees fan." replies Jamie.

A guy calls home from work and a strange woman answers the phone. "Who is this?" he asks.

"This is the maid. I was just hired this morning by the lady of the house," she says.

"This is her husband. Is my wife there?"

"Well, she's upstairs in the bedroom, but I thought he was her husband!" she says.

"What!' the man yells, "How would you like to make $50,000?"

"What do I have to do?" the maid asks.

"I want you to get the gun from my desk and shoot the whore and the jerk she's with. It's justifiable homicide!"

The maid puts down the phone. The guy hears footsteps followed by two gun shots. The maid comes back to the phone and asks, "What should I do with the bodies?"

"Just throw them in the swimming pool," the guy says.

"What pool?" she asks.

"Um-is this 555-9416?"

Brian takes his friend hunting, but when they get to his favorite spot, there is "No Trespassing" signs everywhere. Brian tells his friend to wait in the car and walks up to the farm house and knocks on the door.

The farmer answers the door and Brian says, "Sir, I've hunted on this property all my life, but now I notice that you have a bunch of signs up. I wanted to see if it was still okay for me to hunt here."

The farmer scratches his chin and says, "I'll make you a deal. We've got this cow out back that we have to kill for food, but we've grown too attached to it. If you go out back and shoot my cow, I'll let you hunt on my property."

Walking back to the car, Brian decides to play a joke on his friend. "The old bastard won't let us hunt on his property," he tells him. "I'm going to shoot his cow!" He walks over to the side of the house and BLAM!

Suddenly two more shots ring out behind him and his friend runs up yelling, "I got the cat and dog, too; let's get the hell out of here!"

Q: What did the doe say when she walked out of the woods?

A: "I'll never do that again for two bucks."

Following a nasty car accident, a man's wife slips into a coma. After spending weeks at her bedside, the husband is summoned to the hospital.

"It's amazing," says the doctor, "while bathing your wife, one of the nurses noticed she responded to her breast being touched." The husband is very excited and asks what he can do. "Well,' says the doctor. "If one erogenous zone provokes a response, perhaps the others will too."

So, the husband goes alone into the room and slips his hand under the covers and begins to massage her breast. Amazingly, the woman begins to move and even moan a little. The man tells the doctor who's waiting outside.

"Excellent!" he says." if she responds like that to your finger, I think you should try oral sex too."

Nodding, the husband returns to the room to see what he can do. Within minutes the heart monitor alarms suddenly go off and the medics quickly pile into the room to give emergency treatment.

"What happened?"Shouts the doctor as he desperately tries to find the woman's pulse.

"I'm not sure," replies the husband. "I think she choked."

Q: What do you call two skunks performing 69 or each other?

A: Odor eaters.

After a particularly one-night stand, a man notices that there is a photograph of another man on his conquest's dresser.

"Is this your husband?" he asks nervously.

"No, of course not," she replies, snuggling up to him to go to sleep.

"Your boyfriend?"

"No, silly," she says, giggling and nibbling away at the guy's ear, "Not even close!"

"Is it your dad..your brother?"

"No, no, no!" she answers.

"Well, who the hell is he?"

"That's me before the surgery."

A woman holding a baby gets on the bus. The driver looks at them and says, "Damn! That's the ugliest baby I ever seen!"

In a huff, the woman slams her money into the fare box and sits in the back of the bus. The man seated next to her sees she is distressed and asks her what's wrong.

"The bus driver insulted me!" she screams.

"That's outrageous!" says the man, "He's a public servant and shouldn't be insulting passengers."

"You're right!" the woman says. "I think I'll go up there and give him a piece of my mind."

"That's a good idea," says the man. "I'll hold your monkey."

President Clinton looks up from his desk in the Oval Office to see one of his aides nervously approaching him. "What is it?" asks the president.

"It's this abortion bill, Mr. President. What do you want to do about it?" the aide asks.

"Go ahead and pay it," says the president.

Q: What's the difference between a pigeon and an investment banker?

A: The pigeon can still make a deposit on a Ferrari.

A nun goes to confession, "Forgive me Father," she says. "I used horrible language this weekend."

"Go on," the priest says.

"Well," the nun continues, "I was golfing and hit this incredible drive, but it struck a phone line and fell short after only about 100 yards."

"And so you swore?" the priest asks.

"No," the nun says. "After that, a squirrel ran out and stole my ball!"

"Is that when you swore?" the father asks.

"Well, no," the nun says. "Then, an eagle swooped down and grabbed the squirrel in his talons. As they flew away, the squirrel dropped my ball."

"Then you swore?" the priest asks.

"No," she continues, "the ball fell on a big rock, rolled onto the green, and stopped six inches from the hole."

The priest is silent for a moment and then finally says, "You missed the fucking putt, didn't you?"

A man and his wife are in bed when the wife asks, "Do you think we could renew our vows for our 25th anniversary?"

"Sure," says the man.

The wife smiles and says, "It'll be just like the first time."

"Not exactly," says the man. "This time I'll be the one on the edge of the bed crying and saying 'No, it's just too big!"

A man goes into a gun shop to buy a telescopic rifle sight. The assistant takes one out, points at the window and says, "This baby is so good, you can see right into my house on that hill over there."

The man squints through the sight at the house and starts laughing.

"What's so funny?" asks the puzzled assistant.

"Well, I can see a naked man chasing a naked woman around your house," the man replies.

Snatching the scope away from the man, the assistant looks through it, and sure enough, there is his wife being hotly pursued by a excited young man. Furious, the assistant says to the man, "If I give you two bullets, will you blow my wife's head off with one and the man's dick off with the other? I'll give you the telescopic sight for free if you do it."

"Okay," the man says. As he attaches the sight to the rifle, taking a quick look through it before loading it, he hands one bullet back. "You know what?" he says, "I think I can do this with one shot."

An angry boss calls his chronically late worker at home, "You were supposed to be here an hour ago!" he yells.

"Sorry boss," the worker says, "but I won't be in today. I have anal glaucoma."

"What the hell is that?" the boss asks.

"It means I can't see my ass coming to work."

Two women are playing golf on a sunny afternoon when one of them accidentally slices her shot into a foursome of men. To her horror, one of the men collapses in agony, both hands in his crotch. She runs down to him, apologizing, and explained that she is a physical therapist and can ease his pain.

"No thanks... just give me a few minutes...I'll be fine," he says quietly, hands still between his legs.

Taking it upon herself to help the poor man, she gently undoes the front of his pants and starts massaging his genitals. "Doesn't that feel better?" she asks.

"Well, yes...that's pretty good," he admits. "But my thumb still hurts like hell."

An American, a Japanese man and a Canadian are hanging out when suddenly there's a beeping sound. The American says, "That's my pager. I got a microchip under the skin of my hip."

A few minutes later, the Japanese guy lifts his palm, to his ear and says, "It's my new cell phone, I got a microchip in my hand."

The Canadian, not wanting to be out done and wanting to do something more impressive, goes to the bathroom and returns with a piece of toilet paper hanging from his butt. He says, "I told them to send me an e-mail, not a fax."

The madam of a brothel has a problem and goes to a local priest. "I have two talking parrots," she starts to tell him. "All they can say is, "Hi, we're prostitutes. Do you want to have some fun?"

"That's awful,' says the priest. "But I do have a solution to your problem. I have two male parrots who I've taught to pray and read the Bible. We can put your parrots with mine, and I believe yours will stop saying that awful phrase and instead will start reciting the word of God."

The next day, the madam takes her parrots to the priest's house and puts them in with the male parrots that are holding rosary beads and praying in their cage.

"Hi, we're prostitutes," says the female parrots. "Do you want to have some fun?"

One male parrot looks at the other and says, "George, close the Bible, our prayers have just been answered!"

A city boy asks a farmer for his daughter's hand in marriage.

"Prove you are worthy," says the farmer. "Go screw that cow out in the field."

"Anything for her." The kid screws the cow and returns. "Now can we get married?" he asks.

The farmer pointed to a goat and when the boy's done with the goat, he points to a pig.

"You can marry her," the farmer says.

"Screw that," says the city boy. "How much for the farm?"

Herb decides to propose to Sandy, but prior to her acceptance, Sandy had to admit to her man about her childhood illness. She informed Herb that she suffered from a disease that left her left breast at the maturity of a 12 year old.

He stated that it was OK because he loved her so much.

However, Herb felt it was time to tell her about his deformity as well. He looked Sandy in the eye and said, "I too have a deformity. My penis is the same size as an infant and I hope you can deal with it once we are married."

She said "Yes, I will marry you and learn to live with your infant-size penis."

Sandy and Herb got married and could not wait for the honeymoon. Herb whisked Sandy off to their hotel suite and they started touching, teasing and holding each other. As Sandy put her hands in Herb's pants, she began to scream and run out of the room.

Herb ran after her to find out what was wrong.

"You told me your penis was the size of an infant." she said.

"It is," he replies, "8 pounds, 7 ounces and 19 inches long."

Q: What is 6 to 9 inches long, goes in and out of your mouth and leaves white stuff dripping down your lips?

A: A toothbrush.

A woman goes to a tattoo parlor and asks the artist to tattoo a picture of Robert Redford on one upper thigh and a picture of Paul Newman on her other upper thigh.

The artist does this and when he's done, hands her a mirror so she can inspect the work.

She looks at her right thigh and says, "Wow! That's definitely Paul Newman. Just look at those blue eyes." Then she looks at her left thigh and complains, "That doesn't look like Robert Redford."

The artist disagrees and says they need to find an impartial judge. They go to the bar next door and ask the first guy they meet to identify the tattoos. She raises her skirt and drops her panties, and he gets his face up close and says, "Well ma'am; the one on your right thigh is definitely Paul Newman. He even has the blue eyes. The one on your left, I'm not sure about. But the one in the middle is definitely Willie Nelson."

"What's wrong; with me, doc?" asks the patient. "My balls have turned blue. You gotta help me."

The doctor examines him and concludes his testicles will have to be removed or he will die.

"Are you nuts?" the patient cries. "I can't let you do that!"

"Do you want to die?" the doctor asks and the patient has his testicles removed.

Two weeks after the operation, the patient goes back. "Doc, I don't know how to say this, but now my penis has turned blue." The doctor examines him again but reaches the same sad conclusion, if the man wants to live, his penis has to go.

Now the man is crying. "But how will I pee?"

"We'll install a plastic pipe," says the doctor. "You don't want to die do you?"

The man has his penis removed and everything is fine for a while. Two weeks later, he's back at the doctor's office. "Doc, the plastic pipe has turned blue, what the hell is happening to me?"

"Well, I can't quite figure it out," admits the doctor. "Wait, do you wear jeans?"

Q: What's the difference between a banker and a cheese pizza?

A: A cheese pizza can feed a family of four.

For his birthday, a boy wants a bicycle.

His father says "Son, we'd give you one, but the mortgage on this house is $300,000. There's no way we can afford it."

The next day the father sees the boy heading cut the door carrying a suitcase so, he asks, "Son, where are you going?"

The boy says, "I was walking past your room last night and heard you telling mommy you were pulling out. Then, I heard her tell you to wait because she was coming too. I'll be damned if I'm staying here all by myself with a $300,000 mortgage and no damn bike."

A cop pulls over a driver for running a stop sign.

The driver gives the officer a lot of bull and starts to argue that he did stop fully.

The cop says "No sir, you only slowed down."

The guy replies, "Stop or slow down, what's the difference?"

The cop then pulls the guy out of his car and starts to beat him over the head with his nightstick for about two minutes and then calmly asks the driver, "Now, would you like me to stop or just slow down?"

Three blondes were walking in the forest one day when they came across a set of tracks and started to argue over what kind of tracks they were.

The first blonde said, "I think they are deer tracks."

The second blonde said, "I think they are dog tracks."

The third blonde said "1 think they are cow tracks."

They were still arguing over what kind of tracks they were when the train hit them.

Q: What's the difference between a professional cornhusker with epilepsy and a prostitute with dysentery?

A: Well, one shucks between fits.

A third grade teacher says, "Class, today I would like one of you to try to use the word "definitely" in a sentence."

A little girl raises her hand and says, "The sky is definitely blue."

"Not exactly," the teacher answers. "Sometimes the sky is gray and at night the sky is black. Can anyone else use the word definitely in a sentence?"

Another student raises his hand and says, "Leaves are definitely green."

"Close," the teacher says. "But in the fall they turn brown. Anyone else?"

A kid in the back raises his hand and asks, "Are farts lumpy?"

"No." the teacher responds.

The kid replies, 'Then I definitely just shit my pants."

A blonde who suspects her boyfriend is cheating on her goes out and buys a gun. She goes to his apartment unexpectedly, opens the door and sure enough, there he is in the arms of another woman. Now she's angry. She opens her purse and pulls the gun out. As she does this, she is so overcome with emotions she puts the gun to her own head.

The boyfriend yells, "No baby, don't do it."

"Shut up," she says, "You're next."

A woman comes home wearing a gold necklace.

"Where did you get that necklace?" her husband asks.

"I won it in a raffle at work. Now go prepare my bath."

The next day, the woman comes home wearing a diamond bracelet.

"Where did you get that bracelet?" the husband asks.

"I won it in a raffle at work. Now go prepare my bath." she replies.

The day after, the woman comes home wearing a mink coat.

"I suppose you won that in a raffle at work?" the man asks.

"Why yes," the wife says. "Now go prepare my bath."

When the wife goes to take her bath, she notices something strange. "There's only an inch of water in the tub!" she yells.

"Yes," the husband says. "I didn't want you to get your raffle ticket wet."

Q: If you have big boobs you work at Hooters. If you have one leg, where do you work?

A: IHOP.

Mr. Johnson and his secretary are on an international flight in first class.

As they are nodding off for the night, the secretary, who's had a long crush on her boss, says in her best seductive voice, "I'm a little cold. Can I get under your blanket?"

Reading her signals clearly, the boss says, "How would you like to be Mrs. Johnson for a while?"

"I'd love it!" the secretary replies, jumping at the chance.

"Great," Mr. Johnson says. "Then get your own damn blanket."

A drunk gets up from the bar and heads to the bathroom. A few minutes later, a blood-curling scream fills the bar. The bartender runs to the bathroom door and yells, "What the hell is going on in there?"

"I was sitting on the toilet," the drunk says, "and when I flushed, something came up and squeezed the hell out of my balls!"

The bartender opens the door and see's the drunk and says, "You idiot! You're sitting on the mop bucket!"

A chicken and an egg are sitting at a bar having a few drinks. After a few hours, a drunken patron approaches them, "So who came first?" he says grinning at his cleverness.

The chicken glances at the egg, then turns to the drunk and says, 'Your mother."

At the end of a job interview, the head of the human resources department asks the young man

fresh out of MIT, "What kind of starting salary are you looking for?"

The young man decides to shoot for the moon and says, "I'm thinking in the range of about $125,000 a year or so depending on the benefits package."

"Hmm," says the interviewer. "Well, what would you say to five weeks vacation, 14 paid holidays, full medical and dental, a retirement fund with the company matching up to 50 percent of salary and a company car leased every two years, say a Porsche?"

The young man gapes and asks, "Wow! Are you kidding?"

"Yeah," the interviewer says, "but you started it."

A guy walks into a bar with the side of his face bruised and bleeding.

The bartender asks, "What happened to you?"

The guy replies, "I got into a fight with my girlfriend because I called her a cheap hooker."

"What did she do?" asks the bartender.

"She hit me with a bag of quarters."

A nerdy little accountant is sent to jail for embezzlement and put in a cell with a huge bruiser.

"I wanna have sex," the brute groans. "Are you gonna be the husband or wife?"

"Well," croaks the trembling nerd, "If I have a choice, I guess I'll be the husband."

"Ok," the bruiser says, "now get over here and suck your wife's dick."

Q: What sexual position guarantees the ugliest baby?

A: Go ask your mother.

A little old lady goes to the doctor and says, "I can't stop passing gas. Luckily, my farts don't smell and are always silent. As a matter of fact, I've farted twice since I been here in your office and you haven't even noticed."

"I can help you," the doctor says. "Take these pills and come back next week."

The next week, the lady returns. "Doctor," she says. "I don't know what you gave me, but now my farts reek."

The doctor says, "Good, we fixed your sinuses! Now let's work on your hearing."

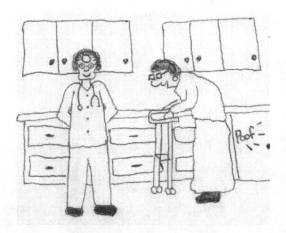

A man and his wife are lying in bed when the man starts to caress the wife's back.

"Not tonight dear," she says. "I have an appointment with the gynecologist tomorrow."

The husband rolls over and tries to go to sleep. A few minutes later, he turns back over and again, starts to caress his wife's back.

"Honey, stop," she says. "I told you I have to go to the gynecologist tomorrow morning."

"I know," he says. "But you don't have to go to the dentist, do you?"

A man asks his friend, "How many legs are there all together on three roosters?"

"Uh, six!" the friend says.

"How many beaks are there on four roosters?"

"Uh, four!" the friend says.

"Well, then, how many wings are there on 12 roosters?" "Come on, there's 24!"

Ok smart guy, how many teeth are there in a cat's mouth?" "

Come on dude, I got no idea."

"How come you know a whole lot about cocks and nothing about pussy?"

A young man takes his blind date to the amusement park for their first date. They go for a ride on the Ferris wheel, but the girl seems bored.

"What would you like to do next?" he asks her.

"I wanna get weighed," she says.

So the young man takes her over to the weight guesser. "One-thirty," says the man and she gets on the scale and proves him right.

Next they ride the roller coaster. Then, they get something to eat and he asks her what else she wants to do.

"I wanna get weighed," she says.

I really struck out tonight the young man starts to think and claims he has a headache and takes the girl home.

The girl's mother is surprised to see she's home so early and ask the girl, "What's wrong, didn't you have a nice time tonight?"

"Wousy," says the girl.

Q: What's the difference between your wife and your job?

A: After five years, your job still sucks.

A man gets home, screeches his car into the driveway, runs into the house, slams the door and shouts, "Honey, pack your bags! I just won the damn lottery!"

"Oh, my God!" she screams. "What should I pack, beach stuff or mountain stuff?"

"It doesn't matter," the husband yells back. "Just get the fuck out!"

A guy gets home from work one night and hears a voice in his head that says, "Quit your job, sell your house, take your money and go to Vegas." The man is disturbed at what he hears and ignores the voice. The next day however, the same thing happens. The voice tells him, "Quit your job, sell your house and take your money and go to Vegas."

Again the man ignores the voice, but he is becoming upset. The third time he hears the voice, he gives in. He quits his job, sells his house and takes all his money to Las Vegas.

The second the man gets off the plane, the voice tells him, "Go to the MGM Grand."

He hops in a cab and rushes to the casino, where the voice tells him, "Go to the roulette table."

The man does as he's told. When he gets to the roulette table, the voice tells him, "Put all your money on 17."

Nervously, the man cashes in all his money for chips and puts it all on 17.

"Now watch," says the voice.

The dealer wishes the man good luck and spins the roulette wheel. Around and around the ball goes. The man anxiously watches as the ball slowly looses speed and settles into a number...21.

The voice says, "Fuck."

Barack Obama visits a classroom and asks the kids if they have questions. A little girl raises her hand and says, "A horse, a cow and a deer all eat grass. But a deer poops pellets, a cow makes patties, and horses crap piles in dried grass. Why is that?"

Obama thinks about it and finally admits, "I have no idea."

The little girl replies, "Ok, second question: Do you really feel qualified to run the country when you don't know shit?"

Q: How many midgets does it take to screw in a light bulb?

A: None. Midgets have night vision, they don't use light bulbs.

What personal-ad lingo really means:

Adventurous: Will sleep with your friends
Athletic: No tits
Contagious: Does lots of ecstasy
Emotionally secure: Heavily medicated
Friendship first: Reformed slut

Three little old ladies are sitting on a park bench one afternoon

when suddenly, a young man in a trench coat runs up and flashes them. Two have a stroke and one can't reach!

Three cowboys, one from Oklahoma, one from Kansas, and one from Texas are sitting around a camp fire.

The Oklahoma cowboy brags, "Just the other day, a bull gored five men in the corral and I wrestled it to the ground with my bare hands."

The cowboy from Kansas says, 'Oh, yeah? Just the other day a 20 foot rattler came at me so, I grabbed it, bit its head off and spit the poison into a spittoon 20 yards away."

The Texan stays quiet, slowly stirring the coals of the fire with his penis.

Twelve seminary students are about to be ordained as priests. For the final test, they lined up in a line, naked. Each priest had a bell attached to his penis. A naked woman came into the room. The head of the seminary told them that anyone whose bell rang would not be ordained as he had not reached a state of spiritual purity.

The woman danced in front of the first student; his bell did not ring. She proceeded down the line with no ringing until she reached the last student. As she danced in front of him, his bell began to ring so loud and hard, that it flew off his dick and fell to the ground. Embarrassed, he bent over to pick it up; then, all the other bells started ringing.

Q: What do panty hose and Osama Bin Laden have in common?

A: They both irritate bush.

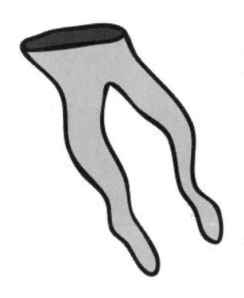

An old man goes to the Social Security office to apply for benefits, but forgets his ID.

The social worker says, "Just unbutton your shirt."

The old man does so, and the social worker says, "The gray hair on your chest is all the proof I need," and gives him his check.

The man tells his wife who says, "If you'd have dropped your pants, you could have gotten disability too!"

A young couple is golfing one day on a very nice course lined with million-dollar homes all around it. On the fourth tee, the husband slices his shot right through the window of the biggest house along the course. They walk up, knock on the door and hear a voice say, "Come on in."

Opening the door, they see glass everywhere and a broken bottle lying on the floor.

A man on the couch says, "Are you the people who broke my window?"

The husband begins to apologize, but the man cuts him off. "Actually, I wanted to thank you. I'm a genie who's been trapped in that bottle for years. Your wayward shot freed me. I'm allowed to grant three wishes to the one who frees me, so, what I'd like to do is grant each of you one and keep the last for myself.

"Fantastic!" the husband says. "I want a million dollars a year for the rest of my life."

"No problem," says the genie, "It's the least I could do. And ma'am, what do you want?"

"I want a house in every country in the world," says the wife."

Consider it done," the genie says, turning back to the man. "And now for my wish. Because I've been trapped in that bottle for so long, I haven't had sex in a long time. My wish is to sleep with your wife."

The husband takes a long look at his wife and says, "Well, we did get a lot of money and all those houses. If you don't mind honey, neither do I."

The wife agrees and the genie takes her upstairs and has sex with her for four hours. After he's through, he rolls over, looks at the wife and asks, "How old is your husband, anyway?'

"Thirty-five," she says.

"And he still believes in genies?"

There is a millionaire who raises alligators in his swimming pool and also has a very beautiful daughter. One weekend he decides to throw a party at his house.

During the party, the host announces, "I will give $1 million dollars or my daughter to the man who can swim across this alligator filled pool and emerge on the other side unharmed!" Just as the millionaire finishes speaking, there's a loud splash in the pool. Everyone turns to see a man swim with all his might and make it to the other side unharmed.

The impressed host asks, "Do you want the million or my daughter?"

"I don't want your money or your daughter," the soaked party guest says, "I want the asshole who pushed me in!"

The New York mafia hires a deaf-mute man to collect its protection money figuring he can't snitch if he gets caught. In his first week, the collector gets more than $50,000. The second week, he stashes the money and tries to leave town, but the mafia guys catch him first and get an interpreter to question him.

"Ask him where he put the money," says the don.

The interpreter signs, "Where'd you hide the money?"

The collector signs back, "I don't know what they are talking about."

The interpreter tells the don, "He says he don't know what you are talking about."

The don pulls out a .38 and put's it to the deaf guy's ear. "Now ask him if he knows what I'm talking about."

The deaf man is frantically signing, "It's in Central Park, in the third tree stump on the right from the East 81st entrance."

The interpreter says, "He still don't know what you're talking about and that you don't have the balls to pull the trigger."

A 90-year old man on his deathbed looks up to his 88 year old wife.

They have been married for more than 60 years and have four sons. Three of the sons have blonde hair and blue eyes. The fourth son, the youngest, has black hair and dark eyes.

The old man asks his wife, "Tell me before I die, is our youngest son my child?"

His wife says, "I swear to you on the Holy Bible that he is your son."

The man smiles, closes his eyes and dies.

The wife turns to the nurse next to her and says, "Thank God he didn't ask me about the first three."

A man walks into a pharmacy and asks the pharmacist for a pack of condoms.

Paying for them, he burst out laughing and walks out of the pharmacy. The next day he comes in again, and again he asks the pharmacist for a box of condoms and again walks out laughing.

Thinking this is very strange, the pharmacist tells his assistant to follow the man if he comes back again.

A few days later, the man comes back into the pharmacy, buys some more condoms and walks out laughing. The assistant follows the man and 20 minutes later, comes back.

"So, did you follow him?" the pharmacist asks.

"Sure did."

"Where did he go?"

"Your house."

An elephant and an ant share a night of ecstasy together. The next morning, the ant wakes up to find the elephant dead. "Damn it," says the ant, "One night of passion and I spend the rest of my life digging a fucking grave."

Q: What's the most successful pickup line ever?

A: Does this smell like chloroform?

A woman goes in for a face lift and the doctor says, "We've got this new method, I put a knob in the back of your head and every time you feel you need a lift, just turn it."

The woman gets the knob implanted and is beautiful for five years. But one day she notices a problem and returns to the doctor. "I've got these huge bags under my eyes," she complains.

The surgeon replies, "Those aren't bags, those are your breast."

"Ah," she sighs. "That explains the goatee."

Walking past the big wooden fence around the insane asylum, a guy hears everyone inside chanting, "Fourteen! Fourteen! Fourteen!" His curiosity going wild, he finds a hole in the fence and looks inside. All of a sudden a finger shoots through the hole and pokes out his eye and the inmates start shouting, "Fifteen! Fifteen! Fifteen!"

A man at a job center in Denver sees an ad for a gynecologist's assistant. Interested, he asks the clerk for details.

The clerk explains, "The job entails helping women cut off their underwear and washing their private areas so they're ready for the exam. The salary is $75,000 and you'll have to go to Montana. That's about 450 miles away."

"Relocate? No problem. I'll go pack my bags!"

"No need to pack sir, that's just where the end of the line for the job starts."

A guy walks into a bar and see's a sign that reads, HAMBURGER $1.00, CHEESEBURGER $2.00, HAND JOB $10.00.

He calls an attractive blonde behind the counter.

"Can I help you?" she asks with a knowing smile and a wink.

"I was wondering," the man says, "are you the one who gives the hand jobs?"

"I sure am," she purrs.

"Well, please wash your hands," he says. "I want a cheeseburger."

A psychiatrist seeing a new patient gets the patient seated comfortably on the couch and starts the session. "I'm not aware of what your problem is," the doctor says. "Why don't you just start at the beginning."

"Of course," the new patient says. "In the beginning, I created the Heavens and the Earth."

During a man's annual physical, the doctor asks him to drop his pants and put his hands on the examination table.

A few seconds into the rectal exam, the man cries out, "Oh, my God!"

The doctor asks him what could be the problem.

The patient says, "The last doctor I went to did this with both his hands on my shoulders."

A young girl walks into a pet store and taps the owner on the shoulder.

"Excuthe me, mithter," the tyke says. "Do you have any widdle wabbits?"

With his heart melting, the owner bends down on his knees and asks, "Do you want a widdle white wabbit or a thoft and fuwwy bwack wabbit? Or how about this widdle hrown wabbit Wight here?"

The little girl responds, "I don't fink my pet python weally gives a thit."

A guy calls a law office and says, "I want to talk to my lawyer."

The receptionist says, "I'm sorry, but he died yesterday."

The next day, the same guy calls the same law office and asks to speak to his lawyer.

The receptionist says, "I told you yesterday, he died."

The next day the guy calls again to talk to his lawyer.

Now the receptionist is getting mad and says, "I keep telling you, your lawyer is dead. Why do you keep calling?"

The guy says, "I just love to hear you say it."

Q: How do you know if you're really ugly?

A: Dogs close their eyes while humping your leg.

A banker in the Old West is on a train when he gets the sudden urge to take a dump. He wants to hold it, but realizes he can't. Being alone in the car and not wanting to mess himself, he pulls his pants down, sticks his butt out the window and proceeds to go number two on the prairie.

Meanwhile, two bandits walking beside the tracks see the train coming toward them quickly.

One bandit nudges the other and says, "You see that chubby guy sticking his head out of the window? Slap him in the face and I'll grab his cigar."

A boy goes to the store and asks, "May I have some light bulbs please?"

"I don't think you own a lamp," the store owner says. "So, the answer is no."

With that, the boy runs home, unplugs the light in his room and rushes it back to the store. "Here's my lamp," the kid says. "Now give me those bulbs."

The store owner complies.

The next day, the boy returns and asks the same man for some cat food. The owner replies, "I don't think you own a cat, so I refuse to sell you cat food."

The boy leaves and comes back with his cat. "Look," the boy says. "Now give me some cat food!"

The owner sells it to him.

A day later, the boy comes in with a paper bag. He says to the owner, "Stick your hand in here, mister."

The man does and the boy asks, "How does that feel?"

"Like shit," the owner replies.

"Exactly," the boy says. "Now give me some toilet paper!"

A woman's car breaks down near a farmhouse. She goes up to the house and knocks on the door. When the farmer answers, she says to him, "My car has broken down. It's Sunday night. Can I stay here just for tonight until tomorrow when I can get some help?"

"Yes you can, ma'am," the farmer says. "But I don't want you messin with my sons, Jimmy and Sammy."

After everyone's gone to bed, the woman quietly goes into the teenager's room and says, "I'm going to teach you the ways of the world. I don't want to get pregnant so you'll have to wear condoms." She puts condoms on the boys and the three of them go at it all night long.

Forty years later, they are sitting on the porch in their rockers and one says to the other, "Remember that woman who came by here years ago and showed us the ways of the world?"

"Yes," Sammy says.

"Do you care if she gets pregnant?"

"Nope," says Sammy. "I guess not."

Me neither so, let's take these things off."

Q: What's the difference between Beer Nuts and Deer Nuts?

A: Beer Nuts are about $3.29 a can. Deer nuts are under a buck.

P. Diddy goes to the doctor and says, "Doc, I've got a problem. Every time I look in the mirror, I get aroused."

"I'm not surprised," the doctor says. "It's because you're a pussy."

One night, a woman walks into a bar in Dallas and sees a cowboy with his feet propped up on the table. He has the biggest feet she has ever seen. "Is it true what they say about men with big feet?" she asks.

"Why don't you come back to my place and find out for yourself?" the cowboy says.

The woman is curious so, she spends the night with the cowboy. The next morning, she hands him $200.

"Well, thank you ma'am," the cowboy says. "Nobody has ever paid me for my services before."

"Don't be flattered," the woman says. "Take the money and buy yourself some boots that fit."

One day a little old lady answers a knock on her door. She is greeted by an energetic salesman carrying a vacuum cleaner. "Morning ma'am," the salesman says. "If you don't mind, I'd like to take a couple minutes of your time to demonstrate the very best in vacuum cleaners."

"Get out of here!" the old lady yells. "I haven't got any money." The old lady tries to close the door, but the salesman quickly wedges his foot in the door and forces his way inside.

"Don't be so hasty!" the salesman says. "At least watch my demonstration." And with that, he empties a bucket of horse manure onto her hallway carpet.

"If this vacuum does not remove all traces of this manure from your carpet," he says. "I will personally eat the remainder."

"Well, I hope you got a damned good appetite," the old lady says, "because they just cut my electricity off this morning."

Q: What is 14 inches long and hangs in front of an asshole?

A: A lawyer's tie.

Two tall trees, a birch and a beech, stand alone in the woods away from the other trees. A sapling

starts to grow between them. The beech says to the birch, "Is that tree the son of a beech or a son of a birch?"

The birch says he cannot tell.

Just then, a woodpecker lands on the sapling.

The beech says, "Woodpecker, you are a tree expert. Can you tell if that's a son of a birch or a son of a beech?"

The woodpecker takes a taste of the small tree and says, "It is neither a son of a beech nor a son of a birch. That, my friend, is the best piece of ash I have ever put my pecker in."

A 95-year-old man and his 94-year-old wife go before a judge seeking a divorce after 75 of marriage.

The judge asks, "Why would you wait 75 years to get a divorce?"

"Well, Your Honor," the old man begins, "we decided to wait until the kids were dead."

Q: What do men and money in the bank have in common?

A: Both lose interest after withdraw.

A man is stopped in heavy traffic in Los Angeles and thinks, "Wow, this traffic is worse than it usually is. We haven't moved in ten minutes." Noticing a police officer walking down the road between the cars, the man rolls down his window and says, "Officer, what the hell is going on up there?"

"It's O.J. Simpson," the cop says. "He's all depressed and lying down in the middle of the road threatening to douse himself with gasoline and light himself on fire because he doesn't have the money to pay the Goldmans. I'm walking around taking up a collection for him."

The man says, "A collection, huh? How much have you got?" "So far," the cop says. "About ten gallons."

A blind man is riding in his private jet when he feels something is wrong. He makes his way up to the cockpit where he finds his pilot unconscious. He fumbles around and manages to find the radio to call for help.

"Help!" he screams. "I'm blind, my pilot is dead and the plane is flying upside down!"

"Sir, we read you," the tower finally responds back. "But if your blind, how do you know the plane is upside down?"

"Because," the man says. "The shit is running down my back."

Mark and Rob adrift in a life boat see an old lamp floating in the sea. Mark grabs it and starts to rub it and a genie pops out and says she'll grant them one wish. Without even thinking, Mark yells out, "Turn the ocean into beer!"

The genie claps her hands and the ocean turns into beer then she disappears in a puff of smoke. Only the lapping of beer against the hull breaks the stillness.

Rob looks disgustingly at Mark and after a long moment shouts, "You idiot! Now we have to pee in the boat!"

Q: How is sex like pizza?

A: Even when it's bad, you still have to pay for it.

Sergeant major is at a party when a woman approaches him and asks, "Is something wrong?"

"Negative, ma'am," the sergeant major replies. "I'm just serious by nature."

"You know, I hope you don't take this the wrong way, but when is the last time you had sex?"

"1955"

"You really need to chill out and have you some fun. I mean, no sex since 1955??"

She takes him to her room where she "relaxes" him throughout the night.

Once done she says, "Wow, you sure didn't forget much since 1955!"

"I hope not," the sergeant major says glancing at his watch. "It's only 21:30 now."

On Christmas morning, a small boy awakes to find a shiny new bike under the tree. The boy is so excited that he immediately takes his new bike out for a ride.

The kid has only made it a few blocks when a police officer stops him.

"Did Santa bring you that bike for Christmas?" the cop asks.

"Yes, sir!" the boy says with a big smile on his face.

But much to the kid's surprise, the cop starts writing him a ticket.

"Next year, tell him to put a reflector on the back." the cop says.

Furious, the boy asks, "Did Santa bring you that horse for Christmas?"

Playing along with the kid, the officer replies, "Yes he did. Do you like him?"

The boy points at the horse and says, "No, but next year, tell him to put the dick on the bottom."

A bum asks a man for ten dollars.

The man says, "If I give you the money, will you use it to by booze?"

The bum says, "No."

The man asks, "Will you gamble it away?"

The bum says, "No."

Then the man asks, "Will you come home with me so my wife can see what happens to a man who doesn't drink or gamble?"

Q: Why does the Easter Bunny hide his eggs?

A: He doesn't want anybody to know he's screwing a chicken.

A wife comes home and turns on the lights. They begin to flicker then go out completely.

"Baby," she says to her husband, "Can you fix the lights?"

The husband replies, "What do I look like, the electrician?"

The husband then goes to the bar and when he gets home, the lights are working just fine. "Who fixed the lights?" he asks his wife.

His wife says, "I asked the neighbor and he said he'd do it for a blow job or a cake."

The husband asks, "Well, what kind of cake did you make him?"

The wife calmly answers, "Who do I look like, Betty Crocker?"

A man and his wife are in the shower together when the doorbell rings. The wife puts on a robe

and goes down to answer the door. It's her husband's friend Will. The woman tells him her husband is in the shower and asks him if he would mind coming back later.

Instead, Will steps in and quietly says to his friends wife, "I have $400 in my pocket. I'll give it to you if you open your bathrobe for me."

She's offended, but really needs the money so she agrees, opens her robe, gives Will a peek and does the robe back up.

Will gives her the $400 and she opens the door for him to leave.

Before he walks out, he says to her, "I have another $400 in my other pocket. I'll give it to you if you let me touch your breast."

Now she's really offended, but she really needs the money so, she opens her robe and lets him touch her breast.

Taking the other $400 from him, she quickly lets him out the door. Going back to the shower with her husband, he asks, "Who was that at the door?"

"Oh, that was just Will," the wife says.

"Will?" the husband says. "That son of a bitch owes me $800!"

A clown and an 8-year old boy are walking through a cemetery in the middle of the night when they both hear a howl in the distance.

The boy turns to the clown and says, "It's dark out here. I'm scared."

"You're scared?" the clown asks, incredulous. "I have to walk back by myself!"

A waiter asks a diner, "'May I take your order, sir?"

"Yes," the man says. "I'm just wondering how you prepare your chicken?"

"Nothing special, sir. We just tell them flat out that they are going to die."

Q: What does a redneck always say just before he dies?

A: "Hey, watch this!"

An 80-year-old man is having a check-up and starts to tell his doctor, "I've never felt better in my whole life. I've got an 18-year-old girlfriend who's pregnant with my child! Tell me what you think of that?"

The doctor then says, "Let me tell you a short story. I know a guy who likes to hike. One day, he was out walking through the woods when a big bear jumped out on him. With no time to think, he pointed his walking stick at the bear and BLAM! The bear drops dead."

"That's impossible," says the old man. "Someone else had to of shot that bear."

"Exactly," says the doctor.

Q: What's the longest sentence known to man?

A: I do.

After the grade school class comes back inside, the teacher asks Alice, "What did you do at recess?"

Alice says, "I played in the sand box."

"That's nice, Alice." the teacher says. "Now Alice, if you can go to the blackboard and write sandbox correctly, I'll give you a fresh baked cookie.

Alice does just that and gets the fresh baked cookie.

Then, the teacher asks Robby what he did at recess.

"I played baseball with the other kids." Robby says.

The teacher says, "Good. If you can write baseball on the blackboard, I'll give you a fresh baked cookie."

Billy writes the word and gets his cookie.

The teacher then asks Mustafa Abdul what he did at recess.

"I tried to play baseball with Billy and his friends, but they threw rocks at me."

"They threw rocks at you? That sounds like blatant racial discrimination!" the teacher says. "If you can go to the blackboard and write blatant racial discrimination, I'll give you a fresh baked cookie."

Three mothers are in a psychiatrist office. The psychiatrist says to the first mom, "Your obsession with food made you name your kid Candy." He then says to the second mom, "Your obsession with alcohol made you name your kid Brandy."

The third mom grabs her sons hand and says, "C'mon, Dick, we don't have to stand for this shit!"

During a trip to New York, the Pope begs his limo driver to let him drive the car. Unable to say no to his holiness, the driver agrees and gets in the back.

Within a block, the two are pulled over, but when the officer sees who's driving, he calls his sergeant. "Sarge," he stammers. "I stopped someone really important and don't know what to do."

"Is it the mayor?" his sergeant asks.

"No sir, more important."

"The governor?"

"Negative sir. More important."

"Don't tell me you stopped the goddamn president!"

"Nope; more important than even the president!" the officer says.

"Who the hell is it then?"

"I don't know," the officer says, "but his driver is the pope!

Muldoon lives with his dog in the Irish countryside. When the dog dies, Muldoon goes to the parish priest. "Father, could you say a mass for the poor creature?"

The father explains, "We can't have services for an animal in the church, but maybe the one down the road will. I heard they are pretty laxed."

"Thanks," says the man. "Do you think $5,000 is enough to donate for the service?"

The father says, "Why didn't you tell me the dog was Catholic?"

A distraught, young woman decides to throw herself into the ocean.

Down at the docks, a sailor sees her crying, takes pity on her and says, "Hey, you've got a lot to live for. You just need a fresh start. I'm off to London in the morning. If you want, I can sneak you on the ship. I'll take care of you and bring you food every day." Moving closer to her, he slips his arm around her and adds, "I'll keep you happy and you can keep me happy."

She agrees and the sailor sneaks her on board the ship that night and hides her in a life boat. Every night for a month, he brings her food and they make passionate love until morning. Three weeks later during a routine search, she is discovered by the ship's captain.

"What are you doing here?" the captain asks her.

"I have an arrangement with one of the sailors," she starts to tell the captain. "He's taking me to London and he's screwing me."

"You bet he is, lady," the captain says. "This is the Staten Island Ferry."

A man says to his doctor, "I'm thinking about having a vasectomy."

"That's a big decision," the doctor says. "You should talk it over with your family."

"I already have," the man says. "They are in favor of it fifteen to seven."

One day, a 10-pound baby is born in the hospital. Oddly, the baby's body weighs five pounds and his balls weigh five pounds. The hospital staff is mystified.

The chief surgeon walks in and asks what is wrong.

The delivering doctor replies, "We don't know what to do with this baby."

The chief surgeon takes one look and says, "You should have him put in a mental hospital."

"Why?" asks the delivering doctor.

"Well, just look at him," the chief surgeon says. "Clearly the boy is half nuts."

The new employee doesn't show up for work on Monday, his first day on the job. Instead, he is calling in sick. He comes in to work the next day and works the rest of the week.

The next Monday, he calls work and says, "I'm sick and won't be in today." Again he come in the following day and works the rest of the week.

He calls in the following Monday and his boss answers the phone. "I'm sick and won't be in." the man says.

"What's the problem?" asks his boss. "I hope you don't plan on calling in sick every Monday."

"No sir, I don't," the man starts to say. "My sister is in a bad marriage and I go over every Monday to console her and next thing you know we end up having sex all day long."

"With your sister??" the boss asks. "That's sickening."

The man says, "I told you I'm sick."

A kindergarten teacher is asking her students what their parents do for a living. When she gets to little Billy, he says, "My father is a piano player in a whore house."

That night, the teacher calls Billy's father and tells him what little Billy said in class and asks for an explanation.

"It's like this," says Billy's father. "I'm really a lawyer, but how are you supposed to tell that to a child?"

A little black kid is in the kitchen helping his mother cook when he spills flour all over himself. "Look mom," the kid says to his mother. "I'm a white kid now."

The mother slaps him up side his head and tells him, "Now, go upstairs like that and tell your father what you just told me. He's going to teach you a lesson."

The kid does as he's told and goes to his father's office, still covered in flour. "Look dad," the kids says to his father. "I'm a white kid now."

The kid's father takes his belt off and whips the kid's ass a few times. "Now," the father says, "Go back down stairs and tell your mother the lesson you learned."

The kid goes back down stairs and his mother asks him, "So, what lesson have you learned?"

The kid, with tears in his eyes, looks at his mother and says, 'I been white for less than five minutes and already hate black people."

A man comes home and finds his wife having sex with another man in his bed.

"What the hell are you doing?" he screams at his wife.

"See," she tells her lover. "I told you he was dumb."

Q: How can you tell a tough lesbian bar?

A: Even the pool table has no balls.

Once upon a time there was an old man who had Alzheimer's. His wife of 50 years loved him dearly, but couldn't take care of him any longer. He would wander around with no clue of where he was or where he was going and sometimes, couldn't remember who he was. She decided to have him put in a nursing home.

At the nursing home, while the wife was filling out the paperwork, one of the nurses told the old man to sit in a chair. The man started to lean to his right and the nurse ran over and put a pillow on his right side to prop him up. A couple of minutes later, the old man starts to lean to his left and the nurse runs over and puts a pillow on his left side. The old man then starts to lean forward and this time the nurse pushes him back and straps him to the chair. Once the wife is done with the paperwork she asks her husband, "So, are you sure this place is okay?"

"It's okay," he says, "but why won't they let me fart?"

At the nursing home one day, the usually happy Mr. Ryan is walking around and looks upset.

One of the nurses notices that Mr. Ryan seems unhappy and asks him what's wrong.

"My penis died." he says.

"You poor thing," the nurse says to him to humor him. "I'm sorry to hear that."

A couple of days later, the same nurse sees Mr. Ryan walking around and he has his penis hanging out of his pants. "Mr. Ryan," she says, "You have to put your penis away. What is wrong with you?"

"Remember, I told you my penis died?" Mr. Ryan says.

"Yes, I do Mr. Ryan." the nurse tells him.

"Well," Mr. Ryan says, "Today is the viewing."

A man stumbles into a bar and hits on every piece of ass in the

place. After striking out several times, he finally sits down next to a beautiful woman and says to her, "Let me buy you a drink."

"First," the woman says to him, "Let me ask you a question. Do you like to have sex?"

"Of course I do!" the man says.

"And do you like to travel?" she asks him.

"I love to!" the man replies.

"Then take a fucking hike." she says.

A man goes to the doctor and tells him that no medicine is helping with his headaches.

"When I get a headache," the doctor says. "I soak in a very hot bath while my wife sponges me off, especially around the forehead. Then, we go into the bedroom, even if I still have a headache, and make love. Instantly the headache is gone. Try it and come back in five weeks."

Five weeks later, the guy returns with a big smile on his face. "It worked, doc!" he says. "I've had headaches my whole life and nothing has ever helped before!"

"Glad to help you out," says the doctor.

"By the way," the man says. "You've got a really nice house."

Two dwarfs go into a bar where they pick up two prostitutes and take them back to their hotel

rooms. The first dwarf is unable to get an erection. His depression is worsened by the fact that from the next room, he hears his little friend shouting out cries of, "Here I come again! One..two..three..uh!" all night long.

In the morning, the second dwarf asks the first, "How did it go?"

"It was so embarrassing." the first dwarf says. "I simply couldn't get a hard-on."

The second dwarf shakes his head. "You think that's embarrassing?" he asks. "I couldn't 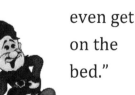 even get on the bed."

Leaving the poker party, late as usual, two friends compared

notes. "I can never fool my wife," the first tells his buddy. "I turn the car off and coast into the driveway, take my shoes off outside, sneak up stairs and undress in the bathroom, but she always wakes up and yells at me for coming in late and leaving her all alone."

"You've got it all wrong, my friend." his buddy starts to tell him. "I roar into the driveway, slam on the brakes and screech my tires, stomp up the stairs, rub my hand on my wife's ass and ask 'how about a little' and she pretends to be asleep."

Q: What did the grain of wheat say the moment it hit the silo?

A: "I've been reaped! I've been reaped!"

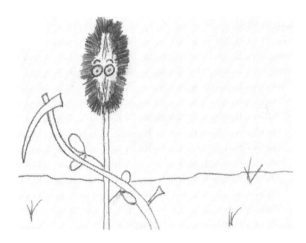

A guy walking along the beach comes across a lantern and rubs it.

A genie pops out and says, "Thank you for releasing me. As a reward, I will grant you one wish."

"Great," says the man. "I want a girl who can cook, a girl who's great looking and a girl who's great in bed."

"Anything else?" the genie asks.

"Yeah, I don't want them to find out about each other."

"Ma'am, are your children twins?" the Wal-Mart greeter asks an ugly woman when she enters the store with her two kids.

"No," the ugly woman tells him. "One son is 9 and the other is 7. Why? Do you think they look alike?"

"No," the greeter says. "I just can't believe you got laid twice."

Q: Why do women fake orgasms?

A: They think we care.

A guy's wife asks him one night, "Baby, if I died, would you re-marry?"

"Well," says the guy. "We all need companionship, so I suppose one day I would."

Well," the wife says. "Would she live in this house?"

"We've spent so much money and time getting this house the way we wanted it," says the man. 'So, I guess she would."

"Would she sleep in our bed?"

"It would be a shame to waste a perfectly good bed," the guy says. "So, I guess she would."

"Would she use my golf clubs?"

"Of course not," the husband says. "She's a lefty."

President Obama gets off Marine One in front of the White House carrying two piglets.

A Marine guard says, "Nice pigs, sir."

The president replies, "These are not pigs, they're authentic Arkansas razorback hogs. I got one for Secretary of State Clinton and one for the Speaker of the House Pelosi."

The Marine says, "Excellent trade, sir."

The C.I.A. is interviewing three potential agents, two men and a woman.

For the final test, they bring one of the male candidates to a door and hand him a gun. "We must know that you will follow every order given to you, no matter what." the interviewer says.

"Inside this room, you will find your wife sitting in a chair; kill her."

"You can't be serious," the man says. "I could never kill my wife."

"Then you're not right for the job." the interviewer says.

The second man is given the same instructions. Five minutes later, he emerges with tears in his eyes and says, "I can't."

Finally, the woman is given the same instructions, only with her husband. She takes the gun and goes into the room. Shots are heard, then screaming, crashing and banging. After a few minutes, she comes out and wipes the sweat from her brow.

"You didn't tell me the gun was loaded with blanks." she says. "I had to beat him to death with the chair."

The morning after their wedding, a husband rolls over and asks his new wife, "Baby, I'm not complaining, but every time we have sex you rub my penis for almost an hour afterwards; how come?"

She rolls over and says, "I don't know. I guess I still miss mine."

A man walks into a bar with his pet alligator and puts the alligator on the bar. Then, he faces the patrons and says, "If I open this alligator's mouth and place my genitals inside, leave them there for five minutes and remove them unscathed, will each one of you buy me a drink?"

The crowd gives its approval so he jumps up on the bar, drops his pants and places his privates in the alligator's mouth. The gator then closes its mouth as the crowd stares in amazement.

After the five minutes, the man gets a beer bottle and hits the alligator on the top of its head. The gator opens its mouth and the man removes his privates unscathed.

The crowd goes wild and his drinks start to come. "Does anyone else have the guts to try it?" the man dares the crowd.

After a few seconds, a blonde woman steps up and says, "I'll do it, just no hitting me on the head with a bottle."

Q: Why doesn't Santa have any kids?

A: Because he only comes once a year and then it's down a chimney.

A guy sees his ex at a bar and tells her "I had wild sex with another woman last night, but thought of you the entire time."

""Oh, do you miss me that much?" she asks him.

"No," he replied, "but it kept me from coming too fast."

Stressed out by city living, a man quits his job and buys a cabin in the woods. His closest neighbor lived four miles away. One night he was finishing his dinner when someone knocks on his door.

"Hi, I'm your neighbor." the man said. "I'm having a party Saturday night and thought you' like to come."

"That sounds great" the man said.

"Gotta warn you though," the neighbor says. "There's gonna be a lot of drinkin."

"I love drinkin." the man says.

"More than likely, there's gonna be some fightin, too." the neighbor heckled.

"I'll just stay out of the way." the man says.

"Last time I had a party, there was some screwing too." the neighbor said.

"Now that's not a problem." the man said. "I've been alone for six months. By the way, what should I wear?"

"Whatever you want." the neighbor said. "Just gonna be the two of us."

A man walks into a bar with an octopus and says, "I bet anyone $50 bucks this octopus can play any instrument you give to him."

A man steps forward with a guitar. The octopus looks at it for a moment, then plays a riff that would stop Hendrix in his tracks.

The next guy hands over a trumpet. The octopus looks at it then plays a tune that Louis Armstrong would envy.

Finally, a guy strolls up and gives the octopus a bagpipe.

The octopus just looks at it perplexed.

Feeling he's about to lose $50 bucks, the octopus' buddy pleads, "Can't you play this thing?"

"Play it?" the octopus says. "If I can get it's pajamas off, I'm gonna screw it!"

Q: How did the electrician lose all the power in his home?

A: He got married.

A blind man walks into a store with his seeing-eye dog. All of a sudden, he picks up the leash and starts swinging the dog over his head.

The manager runs up to the man and asks him, "What the hell are you doing?"

The blind man replies, "Just lookin around."

A man visited the doctor after getting hit in the balls while playing golf. He says to the doc, "How bad is it? I'm getting married next week and my fiancée is still a virgin."

The doctor tells the man, "I'll have to put your penis in a splint to help it heal. It should be ok by next week."

Without telling his fiancée, he marries her on their wedding day.

On their wedding night, she ripped off her dress and took off her bra. She said, "You're the first to see or touch these." Then she took off her panties and said, "No one has ever touched me here either."

Barely able to control himself, the man drops his pants and said, "Look at this; it's still in the crate!"

The ambitious coach of a girls track team starts giving his players steroids. Their performance soars and they go on to win the state championship. The day before the nationals Sara, a 15-year old hurdler comes into his office.

"Coach," she says. "I have a problem I need to talk to you about. I have hair starting to grow on my chest."

"Oh my God!" the coach yells. "How far down does it go?"

"Down to my balls," she says. "And that's the other thing I wanted to talk to you about."

Q: Why does a bride smile as she's walking down the aisle on her wedding day?

A : She knows she's given her last blow job.

An unemployed pianist walks into a piano bar and starts playing great.

The manager runs up to him and tells him he's never heard anyone play that good before.

"Thanks," says the pianist while he starts playing another tune. "I call that one Smell my Balls. This one's called Banging a Bag Lady."

"I'll tell you what," the manager says. "Come by tonight and we'll see how it goes. Just don't tell the name of your songs to my customers."

That night, the pianist quickly gets the place rocking. After playing for an hour, he gets up to go to the bathroom. When he comes back, a hush comes over the crowd.

One of the customers leans over and says, "Hey, buddy, do you know your schlong is hanging out of your zipper?"

"Know it?" says the pianist. "I wrote it!"

A married couple is eating out when the wife notices her ex-husband sitting at the bar.

"He's been drinking like that since I left him seven years ago." she said to her current husband.

"That's silly dear," he replied. "No one celebrates that long."

Officer: "Soldier, do you have change for a dollar?"

Soldier: "Sure, buddy."

Officer: "That's no way to talk to a ranked officer! Let's try that again. Soldier, do you have change for a dollar?"

Soldier: "No sir!"

A truck driver in Death Valley sees something on the side of the road. He pulls over and finds a man hog-tied with tape on his mouth.

When the driver takes the tape of the guy's mouth, the man sputters, "I picked up a hitchhiker and he beat me up, stole my Porsche and kidnapped my wife!"

The truck driver starts to unbuckle his belt and whispers, "Well, buddy, I guess this just ain't your lucky day."

Q: What's the hardest thing about eating a vegetable?

A: The wheelchair.

A man is lying on his deathbed.

His wife sits at his bedside holding his hand and praying.

He looks up and weakly says, "I have something I must confess."

"There's no need to." she tells her husband.

"No," he insist, "I want to die in peace. I slept with your sister, your best friend and your mother."

"I know," she replies. "Now just be still and let the poison work."

Q: Did you hear about the flasher who was thinking about retiring?

A: He decided to stick it out for another year.

An old guy's car collides with a young guy's car and both are smashed up pretty good. The two

crawl out of the wreckage, neither of them hurt.

The old guy says, "Look at this miracle! This is a sign from God that we should meet and be friends and live our lives in peace for the rest of our lives.

"Sure it is," says the young guy thinking the old guy is crazy.

"And look at this!" the old guy says reaching back into his car. "A miracle! My car is demolished, but this bottle of 15-year old scotch didn't break. Surely God wants us to drink and celebrate our good fortune."

Again the young guy agrees so the old guy opens the bottle and passes it to him.

The young guy smiles and takes a couple of huge swigs from the bottle then tries to pass it to the guy who refuses.

Surprised, the young guy asks, "Aren't you having any?"

"No thanks," replies the old guy. "I'll wait for the police."

Satan greets a new arrival in hell by showing him three doors from which he must choose how he'll spend eternity. Behind the first door, there's a man hanging above a pit of fire. The new guy shakes his head and the two move on. Behind the second door, there's a man chained to a wall being tortured. Again the man takes a pass and they go to the third door where an old man is getting head from a beautiful woman.

"Looks good to me," the man says. "I'll take it."

"Great," Satan says. "Lady, your replacement is here."

A man is walking down the beach when he trips over a lamp.

After he rubs it, a genie pops out and says, "I will grant you three wishes, but since you did not treat my lamp with respect, I will give twice what you want to the person you hate the most, your boss."

The man agrees and makes his first wish. "I want a lot of money."

Instantly, $40 million appears in bags on the beach and $80 million appears in his boss' bank account.

Then, the man asks for an incredible sports car. Instantly, a Lamborghini appears and two show up in his boss' garage.

Finally, the genie says, "You have only one wish left, make it worth your while. Remember who else gets double what you ask for."

"Well," the man says. "I've always wanted to donate a kidney."

Q: How can you tell a pig is in heat?

A: She buys the first couple rounds.

A man walks into an incredibly hot doctor's office to get a problem checked out.

"You have to stop masturbating," she tells him.

"Why?" the man asks.

"Because, I'm trying to examine you."

A woman is walking to work one day when she walks past a pet shop that has a parrot perched out front.

The parrot squawks, "Hey, lady! Man are you ugly!"

Pissed, the lady storms past the parrot to work.

On her way home, the parrot spots her again and says, "Hey, lady! Man are you ugly!"

The enraged woman storms into the pet shop to complain. She confronts the manager who apologizes and promises to make sure the parrot doesn't say it again.

When she walks past the store the next morning, again the parrot calls to her, "Hey, lady!"

She pauses and asks, "Yes?"

"You know."

A woman develops a brain tumor and her doctor tells her it could kill her soon. Luckily, he has good news. He has come up with a way to do brain transplants. Unfortunately, there is no donor so, she has to wait.

The next week the doctor calls her and tells her, "You're in luck. There was a terrible accident and two women died - a blonde and a redhead; so, there are two brains available."

"That's wonderful!" the woman says. "Which one should I get?"

"Well, cost is a big factor," the doctor tells the woman. "The redhead's brain would run you $30,000 and the blondes will cost $100,000."

"I don't understand," the woman says. "Why such a difference in price?"

"Well, the redhead's brain is used."

Q: Why doesn't Jesus go into bars?

A: He's afraid to get hammered and hung over.

A woman visits a doctor for a bee sting she got as she golfed.

"What seems to be the problem?" the doctor asks the woman.

"I was stung between the first and second holes while playing golf." the woman tells him.

"Wow," the doctor says. "You must have an awfully wide stance."

A woman is in bed with her lover when her husband walks in the house. "Hurry!" she says. "Stand in the corner."

She rubs him down with baby oil and throws powder all over him. "Pretend you're a statue!" she tells him.

"What's this?" the husband asks as he comes into the bedroom.

"Oh, it's just a statue," she tells him. "The Smiths had one just like it and I liked it so, I bought one too."

Around 3 a.m. the husband gets up, goes to the kitchen and comes back with a sandwich and a beer.

"Here, have this." he says to the statue. "I stood like that at the Smiths for two days and nobody offered me a damn thing."

A Zen master visiting New York City goes up to a street vendor and says, "Make me one hot dog with everything on it."

The vendor fixes the hot dog and hands it to the Zen master who hands the vendor a $20 bill.

The vendor puts the bill in the cashbox and closes it.

"Excuse me, but where is my change?" the Zen master asks.

The vendor responds, "Change must come from within."

Q: What's the difference between a light on and hard on?

A: You can sleep with a light on.

A man is driving in a crowded parking lot looking for a spot to park. He looks up and says, "Lord, if you give me a spot, I'll swear off gambling for life."

Just then, a space appears and the man looks up again and says, "Never mind. I found one!"

An 18-year-old girl told her mother she was pregnant. "And it's all your fault." the young woman said.

"My fault?" the mother asks. "I gave you a sex manual and told you about the facts of life."

"Yeah, yeah," the girl says. "But you never taught me how to give a decent blowjob, did you?"

A man is driving through the hills of Scotland when a big redheaded man steps out in front of his car.

As the driver slams on his brakes, he sees a beautiful young woman standing on the side of the road. When the car stops, the big redheaded man opens the door and drags the driver to the side of the road.

"I want ye tae masturbate!" the big guy shouts. "Dae it noo…or I'll bloody kill ye!"

Terrified, the man drops his pants and does as he's told and starts to masturbate. It doesn't take him long to finish with the girl there.

"Again!" says the big redhead.

The scenario is repeated several more times until the driver rubs himself raw and gets cramps in both his arms. He finally collapses in a sweaty heap on the ground.

"I can't do it again. You'll just have to kill me!" the man cries.

The big redhead looks down and says, "All right, laddie. Now give me daughter a lift to Inverness."

Q: Why don't Ken and Barbie have kids?

A: Because Ken comes in a different box.

"Doctor, could you please kiss me?" asks the patient.

"No, you're a very beautiful woman, but it's against my code of ethics," the doctor tells her.

"Please doctor, just one kiss," she begs the doctor.

"Sorry," the doctor tells her. "It's totally out of the question. I shouldn't even be fucking you."

A man picks up a lamp lying in the street, rubs it and out pops a genie who says he'll give him one wish.

"I wish for tequila whenever I want it." the man says. "I want to pee tequila!"

The genie grants the man's wish and is gone.

When the man gets home, he pisses in a glass. It's the best tequila he's ever tasted. He convinces his wire to drink a glass and she too, loves it.

The two then drink all night long.

The next night, the man tells his wife, "Grab one glass and we'll drink tequila."

"Why only one glass?" the wife asks.

"Because tonight," t he man says, "You drink straight from the bottle."

A young executive is working in the office late one night when he sees the company CEO standing in front of the shredder with a piece of paper in his hand.

"Listen," the CEO says. "This is a very important document and my secretary is gone for the night. Can you make this thing work?"

"Certainly, sir." the young executive says. He then turns the machine on, puts the paper in it and hits the start button.

"Thanks," the CEO says. "I just need one copy."

Q: What do you call a lesbian with fat fingers?

A: Well-hung.

A woman in the super market hurries to the express checkout line with a few items. The clerk has his back towards her so, she says, "Excuse me, I'm in a hurry. Could you please check me out?"

The clerk turns, looks her up and down and says, "Nice tits."

As services were letting out of a Catholic church, a young boy is hit by a car. The driver of the car gets out, horrified. Afraid the boy might die, the driver asks him, 'Do you want me to get the priest?"

The boy opens his eye, looks up at the man and says, 'How can you possibly think about sex at a time like this?"

A man and a woman get in the elevator at the same time. The man asks the woman which floor she wanted.

"The second," she says. "I'm going to the blood bank. They pay $25 to blood donors."

As he pressed the button for the second floor, the man says, "I'm going to the fourth floor. They pay $200 fresh donations at the sperm bank."

A couple of weeks later, the man sees the same woman in the elevator again. "Second floor?" he asks her.

Her mouth full, she just shook her head and held up four fingers.

A woman is driving through Idaho when her car breaks down.

An Indian on horseback comes by and offers to take her to a nearby town. She climbs up on his horse behind him and they ride off. Every few minutes during the ride, the Indian lets out a loud whoop. When they get to town, the Indian lets her off at the local gas station, yells one last time and rides off.

"What did you do to that guy?" the gas station attendant asked her.

"I just put my hands around his waist and held onto the saddle horn so I wouldn't fall off," she said.

"Lady," the attendant says, "Indians ride bareback!"

Q: Why does Kobe Bryant cry after sex?

A: The pepper spray.

After spending the evening at a hotel with a prostitute, a politician puts $500 on the table.

"Thanks," says the prostitute. "But I only charge $50 bucks."

"$50 bucks for the whole night?" the politician asks her. "There's no way you can make a living off that."

"Oh, don't worry," the prostitute tells him. "I do a little blackmail on the side."

A doctor is showing a nursing intern around the hospital. The doctor opens the first examination room door revealing a naked man masturbating.

Embarrassed, the nursing intern declares, "Doctor, that's disgusting!"

The doctor shuts the door and explains, "Mr. Smith has a serious condition. If he doesn't relieve himself four times a day, his genitals swell to a painful size."

The intern calms down a little and the two continue on. The doctor opens the next door to reveal a nurse giving a patient a blowjob.

The intern is shocked. "What the hell is going on in there?"

"That patient has the same condition as Mr. Smith," the doctor starts to explain. "He just has better insurance."

A husband suspected that his wife was having an affair so he hired a famous Chinese private Detective. A few days later he received this note:

"Dear Sir,

You leave house. He come house. I watch. He leave house. She leave house. I follow. He and she go into hotel. I climb tree and look in window. He kiss she. She kiss he. He undress she. She undress he. He play with she. She play with he. I play with me. Fall out of tree. No fee."

Eating pussy is like driving in the fog...if you don't slow down and pay attention you could run into the asshole in front of you.

Timothy O'Connor goes to confession and says, "Father, forgive me for I have sinned."

"What have you done, Timothy O'Connor?"

"I had sex with a girl."

"Who was it, Timothy?"

"I cannot tell you, Father. Please forgive me."

"Was it Mary O'Keefe?"

"No, Father. Please forgive me for my sin, but I really cannot tell you."

"Was it Catherine Sullivan?"

"No, Father. Please forgive me."

"Well then, it has to be Sarah McKenzie?"

"No, Father, please forgive me."

A minute later, Timothy walks out to the pews where his friend is waiting.

"What did ya get?' his friend asks him.

"Five Hail Marys, four Our Fathers and three good leads."

Q: What's the difference between tampons and cell phones?

A: Cell phones are for assholes.

Did you know the Taliban are using sheep to search for land mines?

They send the sheep into the field and if they blow up, the terrorist have dinner. If the sheep make it through, they have a date for the night.

Two men are pulled over for speeding and when the trooper gets to the driver's widow, he taps on it with his night stick. When the driver rolls his window down,--whack!-the trooper hits him in the head with the stick.

"What was that for?" asks the driver.

"Shut up and give me your license." the officer tells him. Then, he goes back to his cruiser, runs a check and returns when the guy comes back clean.

Then, he walks up to the passenger's widow and taps on his window. When the passenger rolls his window down--whack!--the trooper hit him on the head, too.

"Just making your wish come true," the officer tells him.

"What wish?" the passenger asks.

The trooper says, "I know that a couple of miles down the road, you're gonna turn to your buddy and say I wish that asshole would've tried that shit with me."

A cabbie picks up a nun in New York.

About five minutes into the ride, the nun notices the driver staring at her in the rearview mirror.

"Is everything ok, my son?" she asks.

"Everything is fine sister," the cabbie replies.

Another five minutes goes by and he's still staring so, again she asks, "Is everything ok, my son?"

"I want to tell you something, but I don't want to offend you." the driver replies.

"I've heard it all, my son. Speak your mind."

"Well," the driver starts to say. "It's always been a fantasy of mine to kiss a nun."

About a minute passes without either of them saying a word then, the nun replies by saying, "Are you a Catholic and are you single?"

"Yes," the driver says.

The nun tells him to pull over in the next alley where the nun gives him a long two minute kiss. The driver thanks the nun then gets back on the road. The nun notices him crying two minutes later and asks him what is wrong.

"I feel so bad sister and I have a confession to make." the driver says. "I'm a married man and Jewish.'

"That's ok," the nun says. "My names Kevin and I'm on my way to a Halloween party."

Two drunks are walking down the train tracks when one says to the other, "Wow, this is the longest set of stairs I've ever seen in my life."

"It's not the stairs that's killing me," the other drunk says. "It's this low fucking hand rail!"

"Last night I made love to my wife four times," an Italian man brags, "And this morning, she couldn't stop telling me how wonderful it was."

"Last night, I made love to my wife six times," the Frenchman replied, "And today she told me she could never love another man."

The American stayed silent and the Frenchman asked him, "How many times did you make love to your wife last night?"

"Just once," the American says.

"Only once?" the Italian snorted. "And what did she say to you this morning?"

"Don't stop."

Q: What do a near-sighted gynecologist and a puppy have in common?

A: A wet nose.

A woman's business has failed terribly and is in dire need of money so she decides to ask God for help. "God, please let me win the lottery."

Lottery night comes and someone else wins.

The next night, she prays again, "God, please let me win the lottery."

Lottery night comes and again, someone else wins.

One last time she prays, "God, why have you forsaken me? Please let me win so I can get my business back."

Out of nowhere, there is a flash of light and God's voice, "Lady, I'll let you win, but you have to work with me on this. Buy a damn ticket."

A man walks by a house that has a dog tied up outside with a sign that reads, "'Talking dog for sale, $10."

"What's your story?" the man asks the dog.

"Well," the dog says. "When my owner found out I could talk, he signed me up with the C.I.A. and they flew me all over the world on eavesdropping missions. I took down a lot of high-profile targets, won a bunch of medals and eventually retired out here to the country."

Amazed, the man goes inside to ask why he only wants $10 for this amazing dog.

"Because he's a fucking liar," the owner says. "He didn't do any of that shit."

The woman was so blonde:

She took a ruler to bed to see how long she slept.

She thought a quarterback was a refund.

She thought meow mix was a CD for cats.

She told her friend to meet her at the corner of walk and don't walk.

She thought she couldn't use her AM radio in the evening.

She studied for a drug test.

She thought hamburger helper came with an assistant.

She brought toilet paper to a crap game.

When she filled out a job application, in the section for who to contact in case of emergency, she wrote 911.

I told her if she could guess how many quarters I had in my hand, I'd give her both of them. She said three.

Did you hear about the new paint color they have coming out?

It's called blonde. It's not very bright, but it spreads easy.

A distressed man downed several drinks in rapid succession.

The bartender asked him, "You trying to drown your sorrows, buddy?"

"You could say that," the man replies.

"It usually don't work, you know?" the bartender says.

"No shit," the man moans. "I can't get my fucking wife anywhere near the water."

Old Dan's hospital bed is surrounded by well-wishers, but it's not looking good for him. All of a sudden, he motions to the pastor for something to write on. The pastor hands him a pen and piece of paper and Dan uses his last bit of energy to write a note, then dies. The pastor thinks it best not to look at the note right away, so he puts it in his jacket pocket.

At Dan's funeral, as the pastor finishes his eulogy, he remembers he's wearing the jacket he was wearing the day that Dan died. "Dan handed me a note right before he died," he says. "I haven't looked at it, but knowing Dan, I'm pretty sure there's a word of inspiration in it for us all."

Opening the note, he reads aloud, "Help! You're standing on my oxygen tube!"

A man asks a woman at a bar, "Have you ever had magic sex?"

"No." the woman says. "How do you do it?"

"It's easy and fun," he says. "We go back to my place, have sex and you disappear."

Q: What separates five nymphomaniacs from two drunks?

A: The cockpit door.

A man is sitting at a bar alone when he notices a woman sitting at the opposite end alone.

The woman ask him, "You here all by yourself?"

The guy replies, "Yeah, my wife left me because I'm into kinky sex."

The woman says to him, "My husband just left me for the same reason. Why don't we go back to my place and see whose kinkier?"

They go back to her place and when the woman cones out of the bathroom, she's wearing a gas mask and holding handcuffs, but the guy is already halfway out the door.

"Hey, I thought we were going to have kinky sex," she says.

"Well," the guy says, "I fucked your cat and shit in your purse. Thanks for the lovely evening!"

A man on a road trip stopped at a rest area to relieve himself. The first stall in the restroom is occupied so, he goes into the second stall. As soon as he sits down, the guy in the next stall said, "Hi, how's it goin?"

The man thought it was odd to start a conversation in a toilet, but just to be nice said, "Not bad."

Then the voice said, "What are you doing?"

The man replied, "I'm on a road trip."

At this the stranger said, "Look, I'll call you back. Every time I say something to you, the idiot in the next stall keeps answering me."

A whore is like a bowling ball, she gets picked up, fingered and thrown.

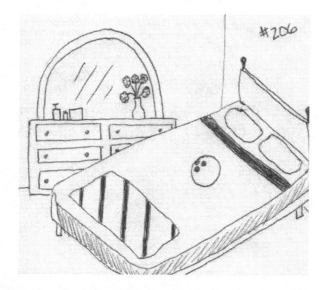

A wife finds her husband standing over their newborn's crib in the middle of the night. As he watches his new son sleeping, she sees on his face a mixture of emotions, disbelief, doubt and amazement. Her eyes glistening, she wraps her arms around him. "A penny for your thoughts," she whispers to him.

"It's amazing," he whispers back to her. "How can anyone make a crib like that for only $39.99?"

Q: Why do police in West Virginia have so much trouble solving murders?

A: Because all the DNA is the same and there are no dental records.

A man is watching a parade in town and is dying to take a leak.

The line for the toilet is long, but he spots a hole in the fence and decides to put it to good use. Midstream, something grabs his dick.

"Give us five bucks or we'll chop off your cock," he hears.

Terrified, he throws five bucks over the fence and is released. Curious, he peeks ever the fence and sees a 12-year old holding a bucket and a huge knife.

"You little bastard, how much have you made today?" the man asks the older kid.

"About $200 bucks." he answers.

"And what about you little kid?"

"I haven't made a cent mister," the younger kid says. "But I do have a bucket full of cocks."

A man sits alone with his soon to be mother-in-law and the dog. The man is so nervous that his stomach begins to hurt and "Pfft." he accidentally lets out a little gas.

He's horrified until the mother-in-law yells, "Rocco!" and the man thinks she thinks it's the dog.

A couple of minutes later, he lets another one rip and the mother-in-law yells, "Rocco!" again.

Feeling confident now, the man lets out a really loud, big, fat, wet one, "Pfffft!"

The mother-in-law yells, "Rocco! Get over here before that pervert shits on you, too!"

Q: What's 50 feet long and smells like piss?

A: A conga line at an old folks' home.

A guy goes to his doctor because he's having a lot of problems remembering things. After a bunch of test the doctor says, "I have bad news and some very had news."

"What's the very bad news?" the man asks worried.

"Well," the doctor says. "Your test shows that you have cancer and only have a couple of weeks to live."

"Oh, my God!" says the man. "What's the bad news?"

"Your test also indicates that you have Alzheimer's disease," the doctor says.

"Well," says the man. "I can always look on the bright side. At least I don't have cancer."

A couple is having sex when their son walks in. He runs out of the room screaming and crying.

The father says, "I better go talk to him." On the way to his son's room, he hears something in his own mother's room, looks inside and is shocked to see his son going at it with grandma. His son looks up and says, "It's not so nice when it's your mom, is it?"

One afternoon, a rabbi sits down on a park bench and begins eating a piece of matzo. After a while, he realizes that the man sitting next to him is blind and takes pity on him. The rabbi breaks off a piece of his matzo and gives it to the man.

Several minutes later, the blind man taps the rabbi on the shoulder and asks, "who wrote this shit?"

The priest of a small village had a pet rooster. One Saturday, he noticed the rooster missing. He suspected it had been stolen to be used in cockfighting. At mass the next morning, he asked his congregation, "Has anyone got a cock?"

All the men stood up.

"No, no," he said. "That wasn't what I meant. Has anyone seen a cock?"

All the women stood up.

"No, no, that wasn't what I meant either. Has anyone seen a cock that doesn't belong to them?"

Half the women stood up.

"No, no," he said. "Perhaps I should rephrase the question. Has anybody seen my cock?" All the choir buys stood up.

An Amish woman was driving her horse and buggy down the road when a cop pulled her over.

"You have a broken reflector on your buggy," the cop tells her. "But the reason I stopped you is because one of your reins is looped around the horse's balls. That could be cruelty to animals. Have your husband fix that right away."

Later that night, the woman tells her husband, "A policeman stopped me today for two reasons. First, he said something about a broken reflector."

"Well, that's easily fixed," the husband says. "What else?"

"I'm not sure. Something about the emergency brake."

Q: How do you make a cat go 'woof'?

A: Soak it in gas and light a match.

A small boy ends up getting lost in a large shopping mall. He

approaches a police officer and says, "Excuse me, officer, but I've lost my grandpa!"

The cop asks him, "What's he like?"

The little boy thinks for a minute then tells the officer, "Peppermint schnapps and women with low self-esteem."

Al despises his wife's cat so he decides to get rid of the cat by driving him 30 miles from home and leaving him in a park. But, when Al gets home, the cat is sitting in the driveway.

The next day, Al drops the cat off 60 miles from home. Again, as soon as he gets back home, there sits the cat.

Al keeps taking the cat farther and farther away and each time, the cat beats him home.

Finally, Al drives the cat over 200 miles from home and leaves the cat there. Hours later, Al calls home to his wife. "Honey, is the cat there?"

"Yes," she says. "Why do you ask?"

Frustrated, Al says, "Could you put him on the phone? I'm lost and need directions back home."

He's 80 and she's 25. It was the talk of the town when an 80-year old man married a 25-year old girl. After a year of marriage, the girl went into the hospital to give birth. The nurses came out to congratulate the old man by saying, "This is amazing, how do you do it at your age?"

"You got to keep the old motor running," he answered.

The next year, the young bride gives birth again.

The same nurse said, "You're amazing, how do you do it?"

Again he tells her, "You gotta keep the old motor running."

The same thing happens the next year.

The nurse then says, "Well, well, you certainly are quite a man."

Again, he tells her, "You gotta keep the old motor running."

"Well," the nurse says. "You better change the oil. This one's black."

Two blondes are working on a house.

One of them, who's nailing down the siding has been reaching into her nail bag, pulling out a nail and would either toss it away or nail it.

The second blonde, wanting to know why she's doing this, goes over and asks her, "Why are you throwing half the nails over your shoulder?"

The first blonde tells her friend, "If I pull out a nail and it's pointed at me, it's defective so, I throw it away. If it's pointed towards the house, then I nail it in."

"You moron," the second blonde yells. "Those nails pointed at you aren't defective. They're for the other side of the house!"

Q: What's the best thing about having an emo lawn?

A: You never have to mow it. It cut's itself.

A pig with three medals around its neck is lying in the dining room while a farmer and his family and a guest are having dinner. Intrigued, the guest asks about the pig.

"He's a special pig." the farmer tells him. "The first medal is for when he dragged our daughter out of a burning barn. The second medal is for when he saved our son from drowning. The third is for pushing our son out of the way of a tractor."

"Wow," the guest says. "That explains all the medals, but how come he has a peg leg?"

"Well," the farmer says. "You don't eat a pig like that all at once."

One day a teacher asked the kids in his class, "If you could have any raw material in the world, what would it be and why?"

Little Hick raises his hand and says, "Gold, because it's worth a lot of money and I could buy a corvette."

Another student, Jenny, answers, "Platinum, because it's worth more than gold and I could buy a big house."

The teacher then asks Steve what he would want. "I would want silicone."

"Why silicone?"

Steve says, "Because my mom has two bags of the stuff and you should see all the sports cars outside our big house!"

After a long night at the bar, a man stood to leave and fell flat on his face. Thinking some fresh air would help him, he crawled outside, but when he tried to stand up outside, he fell again flat on his face into the mud. So, he decided to crawl home.

The next morning, the man's wife finds him asleep on the front porch.

"You went out drinking again, didn't you?" she asked him.

"How did you know?" he asks her.

"Because you left your wheelchair at the bar again."

A bartender is closing his bar for the night when he hears a knock on the back door of his bar. When he answers the door, there is a dirty homeless guy who asks him for a toothpick. The bartender is a little surprised, but gives the man a toothpick. A little while later, there's another knock at the back door. He answers it to find another homeless guy who also asks the bartender for a toothpick. He gives the man a toothpick and he leaves.

A few minutes later, there's another knock at the door and when he answers the door, there is another homeless guy standing there.

"Let me guess, you want a toothpick." the bartender says.

"Actually, no. But can I have a straw?" the homeless man asks him.

The bartender gives him a straw and says, "Two guys wanted toothpicks and you want a straw. What the hell is going on?"

"Well," the homeless man says. "Some drunk girl threw up outside, but all the good stuff is gone.

Q: What's the difference between a good lawyer and a bad lawyer?

A: A bad lawyer can let a case drag out for a couple of years. A good lawyer can make it last longer.

"I was cleaning Father John's room a couple of days ago," one nun says to another, "And I found a box of condoms."

"Oh, my God!" the nun says. "What did you do?"

"I poked holes in them," the first nun says.

"Fuck!" the second nun says.

Two old men are sitting on the porch arguing over who's dog is smarter.

"My dog is practically a genius," the first old man boasts. "Every morning he waits for the newspaper to be delivered, and then he brings it to me."

"I already know," says the second old man.

"What do you mean?" the first old man asks him. "How do you know?"

The second old man replies, "My dog told me all about it."

A lady places a personal ad in the paper that reads, "Looking for a man that won't beat me, run out on me, and is good in bed." Days later, the doorbell rings, and she opens the door to find a man with no arms or legs.

"I'm here about the ad you placed in the paper," he said. "I don't have any arms so, I can't beat you. And I don't have any legs, so I can't run out on you."

"But I need a good lover to." she replies.

"I rang the doorbell, didn't I?"

A penguin is vacationing in America and while he's driving through Arizona, he notices that the oil pressure light is on. He gets out of his car and sees oil spilling out of the engine. He drives to the nearest town and stops at the first gas station he sees.

After leaving his car there to be checked out, he goes for a walk around town. He sees an ice cream shop and, being a penguin in Arizona, decides to get something cold to really hit the spot. He gets a big dish of vanilla ice cream and sits down to eat. Having no hands, he makes a real big mess eating with his little flippers. After finishing his ice cream, he goes back to the gas station and asks it they have determined the problem.

The mechanic looks up and says, "Well, it looks like you blew a seal."

"No, no." the penguin says. "It's just ice cream."

Q: What do Germans use as birth control?

A: Their personalities.

Q: In Mississippi, what do you call a girl who can run faster than her brother?

A: A virgin.

A miner emerges from the hills, walks into a bar and orders a

drink. Looking around, he asks the bartender, "Hey, where, are all the ladies?"

"There aren't any." the Bartender tells him.

"What do y'all do?' the miner asks.

"We do it with the animals," the Bartender tells him.

Disgusted, the miner gets up and heads back into the mines.

Months later, the miner returns to the bar. After downing numerous shots, he asks the Bartender, "Y'all really do it with the animals?"

"Yeah, we do," the Bartender says.

The drunken miner leaves the bar and comes across a pig in the alley. He walks up to it and starts having sex with the pig, which squeals loudly.

Mid way through, he realizes the entire town is watching in horror.

"My God," the Bartender yells. "What the hell are you doing?"

"You told me y'all did it with the animals," the miner says.

"Yeah," the Bartender says. "But nobody fucks the sheriff's girl!"

The hostess of a fancy restaurant walks up and finds two men masturbating furiously by the coat check.

"What the hell do you think you guys are doing?" she screams.

Without looking up or even breaking stride, one of the men points to a sign on the wall that reads, "First come, first served."

A man enters the hospital to get a circumcision. When he comes out after the procedure, the doctor is standing by his bed. "There's been a bit of a mix up," the doctor starts to tell him. "I'm afraid there's been an accident and we were forced to perform a sex-change operation. You now have a vagina instead of a penis."

"What!" the man yells at the doctor. "You mean I'll never experience another erection?"

"Oh, you might," the doctor tells him. "Just not yours."

Two blondes are sitting on the porch talking when one of them sees her husband coming down the street with a bunch of flowers in his hand. She rolls her eye and says to her friend, "Here comes the asshole with flowers in his hand. Now he'll expect me to spend the whole weekend on my back with my legs in the air."

"Why?" her friend asks. "Don't you have a vase?"

A traveling salesman's car breaks down in the country so he decides to call on the closest farmhouse for a place to sleep for the night.

When the farmer opens the door, the salesman says, "Sir, my car broke down just down the road. Could I stay here for the night?"

The farmer says, "Sure, I don't have a problem with that, but you'll have to promise not to sleep with my son."

"Excuse me," says the salesman. "But I think I'm in the wrong joke."

Q: Why did the bald guy cut holes in his front pockets?

A: So he could still run his hands through his hair.

There are four business men having lunch when the first, an American, brags that he has four kids and once he has one more, will have enough for a basketball team.

The Canadian says, "That's nothing, one more and I'll have a hockey team."

The third man, a Japanese man, not to be out done, claims to have eight kids and with the one on the way, he'll have a baseball team.

The last man, an Arab, looks at them and says, "I have 17 wives and one more and I'll have a golf course."

A prisoner who has escaped, breaks into a house and finds a young couple in bed sleeping.

He pulls the guy up, ties him to a chair and then ties the woman down to the bed. He climbs on top of her, kisses her on the cheek and then gets up to go to the bathroom.

While they are alone, the husband tells his wife, "Baby, this guy probably hasn't seen a woman in years. I saw the way he kissed you! If he wants sex, don't resist. Just do what he says and we just might get out of this alive. Be strong baby and remember that no matter what happens, I love you."

"Oh, he wasn't kissing my cheek," the wife says. "He was whispering in my ear. He told me that he finds you incredibly sexy and asked if we keep any Vaseline in the bathroom, but be strong honey, and remember, I love you to."

A little boy and his grandfather are raking leaves in the front yard when the kid spots an earthworm trying to get back in its hole.

"Grandpa," the kid says. "I bet I can put that worm back in its hole."

"I'll bet you $5 bucks that you can't." his grandfather says. "The worm is to wiggly and limp to put it back in that little hole."

The little boy runs into the house and comes back with a can of hair spray. He sprays the worm until it's straight and stiff as a board. The boy then stuffs the worm back in the hole.

The boy's grandfather hands him $5 bucks, grabs the hair spray and runs into the house. Thirty minutes later, his grandfather comes out and hands him another $5 bucks.

"But grandpa, you already gave me five bucks." the kid says.

"I know," his grandfather says. "That's from grandma."

A man is walking down the street when he sees a little boy riding a toy fire engine that's being pulled by a Dalmatian. He sees that the boy has the rope tied around the dogs balls and as a consequence, is pulling the boy very slowly. The man then tells the boy, "You know, you would go a lot faster if you tied the rope around the dogs neck."

"I know," the kid says. "But then I wouldn't have a siren."

Q: What's the definition of embarrassment?

A: Running into a wall with a hard-on and breaking your nose first.

A man comes home and tells his wife that he is going to get a $100 bill tattooed on his penis.

His wife asks him why he would do something so stupid.

"Well," he says. "I like to play with my money. I like to watch my money grow, and if you ever fell like blowing $100, you won't have to go to the mall."

A cop is patrolling lover's lane one night and comes across a young couple sitting in a car. The guy is up front reading a magazine and the girl is in the back knitting. Finding this very odd, the cop knocks on the window and the guy rolls it down.

"Yes, officer?" the man asks.

"I have to ask you," the cop says. "What are you two doing here?"

"I'm reading this magazine, sir," the man says.

"And how about your pretty friend in the back?"

"Well, I think she's knitting a pull-over sweater, sir." the man replies.

"Okay, smart ass, how old are you?" the officer demands, not amused.

"I'm 21, sir." the man tells him.

"And the girl in back?" the officer asks him.

The young man looks at his watch and says, "She'll be 18 in exactly 7 minutes."

A guy goes to his doctor to get some test results. "I have some good news and some bad news for you," the doctor tells him. "Which do you want first?"

"Give me the good news first." the patient says.

"They are going to name a really terrible disease after you."

Q: Why are gypsies so careful when they are making love?

A: Because they have crystal balls.

Sherlock Holmes and Dr. Watson are on a camping trip and fall asleep in their tent. A couple of hours later, Holmes wake up his friend. "Watson, look up at the sky and please tell me what you see."

Watson says, "I see millions of stars."

"And what does that tell you my dear friend?"

Watson thinks this over for a few minutes and then says, "Astromically speaking, it tells me that there are millions of galaxies out there and potentially, billions of planets. Astrologically, it tells me that Saturn is in Leo. What does it tell you?"

Holmes is silent for a minute then says to his friend, "Watson, you idiot! Someone has stolen our tent!"

A wife asks her husband, "Do you love me only because my father died and left me all the money?"

"Of course not," the husband says. "I'd love you no matter who left it to you."

Two lawyers are leaving their office and heading home for the night when the first lawyer says, "I can't wait to get home. As soon as I walk in the house, I'm going to tear my wife's panties off."

"Believe me," the second lawyer says. "I know the feeling."

"No, I'm serious," the first lawyer says. "They're killing me."

Late one night, a man picks up an incredibly hot woman at a bar.

They hop into his convertible and peel off to his house. Desperate to get her home and naked, the man pushes the needle up to 100 mph, but it's still not fast enough for his date. She reaches over from the passenger seat and starts to give him a hand-job. The man becomes so excited that he loses control of himself and his car and ends up running off the road, flips the car and crashes in the woods. A police man comes by and sees that the woman has been thrown from the car, but the driver is still buckled into his seat and alive.

"I'm sorry to have to tell you this," the cop says. "But your girlfriend is dead. You sure are lucky though."

"Lucky?" the guy says. "Go look in her hand!"

A man walks out of the bathroom, naked, and climbs into bed.

His wife says, "I have a headache."

"No problem," he replies. "I was just in the bathroom powdering my penis with aspirin. How would you like it? Orally or as a suppository?"

Three samurai decide to see who is the best swordsman.

A judge approaches the first samurai and opens a box. A fly flies out and the samurai instantly cuts him in half.

"Impressive," the judge tells him before walking over to the second samurai. He opens the second box and when the fly flies out, the second samurai dices it into four equal parts. "Incredible," the judge says.

Finally, the judge opens the third box in front of the last samurai. His sword flashes, but the fly flies away. The samurai just sheaths his sword and smiles.

"But the fly still lives." the judge says.

"Your right," the samurai says. "But he will never have children."

An old man goes into a bar, puts his bad leg over a stool and asks for a shot and a beer. "Hey," he says to the bartender. "Is that Jesus down there?" The bartender nods and the man orders Jesus a beer, too.

An ailing Italian with a hump-back walks in, goes to the bar and asks for a glass of Chianti. Seeing Jesus, he orders him one, too.

A redneck walks in and screams, "Barkeep, set me up a cold one! Hey, is that God's boy sitting there?"

The barkeep nods, so the redneck orders him a beer.

As Jesus gets up to leave, he touches the first man and says, "For your kindness, you are healed!" The man jumps up and starts to dance.

Jesus then touches the Italian and says, "For your kindness, you are healed!"

The Italian's hump-back straightens up and he does a back flip.

Jesus then reaches for the redneck who yells, "Don't touch me! I'm drawing disability!"

Q: Why do bulimics love KFC?

A: Because the food comes with a bucket for them to use later.

A man storms into his house and right up to his wife and tells her,

"You will prepare me a gourmet meal tonight and afterwards we're going to have the weird, kinky sex I've always wanted. And tomorrow, guess who's going to dress me and do my hair?"

His wife looks right at him and says, "The fucking funeral director."

Q: Moms have Mother's Day, and dads have Father's Day. What do single men have?

A: Palm Sunday.

A woman was upset that she hadn't had a date in a while. Her friend suggested she visit a Chinese sex therapist, Dr. Wong. Upon entering his office, Dr. Wong tells her, "Ok, take off your crows." The woman did so and stood there naked.

"Now," Dr. Wong said. "Get down on your knees and crawl very fast away from me to the other side of the room."

She gets down on all fours and does as he says.

"Now, crawl back." he said.

Dr. Wong shakes his head. "Your problem is very bad. You have Ed Zachary disease; worst case I ever seen. That's why you don't have any dates."

Confused, the woman asks him, "What is Ed Zachary disease?"

Dr. Wong tells her "Your face looks Ed Zachary like your ass."

On a duck hunting trip in North Dakota, a big city lawyer shoots a bird and it falls in a field on the other side of the fence. As the lawyer climbs the fence, an old farmer comes up to him and tells him he can't get the bird.

When the lawyer refuses to budge, the farmer tells him, "Here we settle disputes with the 'Three kicks rule' and because the dispute is on my land, first I kick you three times, then you kick me three times and we go on until one of us quits."

The attorney feels he can beat the old man easily so he agrees to the deal.

The old man kicks him in the groin and drops him to his knees. Then, he kicks him in the stomach knocking the wind out of him. Finally, the farmer boots him in the ass.

With a lot of effort, the lawyer stands up and says, "Ok, now it's my turn, old man."

The farmer just smiles and says, "Naw, I give up, you can have the bird."

A chemical fire starts inside a local chemical plant and the alarm goes out to fire departments for miles around. After crews have been fighting the fire for a couple of hours, the chemical company president goes up to the fire chief and says, "All of our secret formulas are in the vault and must be saved. I will give $100,000 to the engine company that brings them out safely!"

All the engine companies try, but not one of them can get through.

Then, another fire truck filled with volunteer fire fighters of men over 50 comes racing down the road and drives right into the raging inferno. The younger men watch as the old men hop off their truck and extinguish the fire, saving the secret formulas.

The company president walks over to reward the volunteers. "What are you guys going to do with all the money?" he asks the group.

The driver looks him right in the eye and says, "The first thing we're going to do is fix the fucking brakes on that truck."

Q: What do you give a man who has it all?

A: Penicillin.

A teacher is testing the senses of her students in class one day. She gives the kids candy and asks them to identify the flavor with a color. Red is for cherry, yellow is for lemon, orange is for orange and green is for lime.

To mix things up a little, the teacher gives them all honey flavored candy. None of the kids are able to identify the flavor so, the teacher says, "Here is one clue for you guys. This flavor is what your parents may sometimes call you."

One little girl looks up eyes wide in horror and screams, "Oh, my God, spit them out! They're assholes!"

A young man has the job of collecting sperm from turkeys to artificially inseminate the other turkeys.

As he comes up on one turkey it said, "Gobble, gobble!"

"Fuck you, dude," the man said. "You're getting a hand-job just like everyone else."

Will and Steve are on a road trip when they end up getting caught in a bad snowstorm. They pull into a farm and knock on the door. A beautiful woman answers the door and they ask her if they can stay for the night.

The woman is sympathetic, but tells them, "I am recently widowed and if I let you stay, my neighbors will talk."

"Then we can sleep in the barn," Will says. "And if the weather improves tomorrow, we'll be gone in the morning."

The woman says they can so they make their way to the barn.

The next morning, the weather has improved, so the men leave.

Nine months later, Will receives a letter in the mail from the woman's attorney. He calls Steve and asks him, "Nine months ago, did you sneak into that widow's room in the middle of the night?"

"Yes I did," Steve tells his friend.

"And did you use my name instead of yours?"

"Yes," Steve replies. "Why?"

"Well, she just died and left me everything!"

As their wedding day approached, a man's fiancée asks him to come over and proof read the wedding invitations. When he walked into the house, his fiancée's beautiful younger sister was standing there.

She whispers into his ear, "I've been in love with you for so long. Before you marry my sister, please make love to me just one time. I'll be upstairs waiting for you."

Stunned, the man walks outside to his car.

The father shakes his head and says, "Me and my daughters put you to a test and you passed. We couldn't ask for a better man to marry into the family."

Moral of the story: Always keep your condoms in the car.

Two drunken Canadians are sitting in a bar and decide to play twenty questions. The first Canadian tries to think of a subject for his friend to guess and finally comes up with, "moose cock." He tells his friend he's ready.

"Ok," his friend asks, "Is it something good to eat?"

The first Canadian thinks for a minute then says, "Yeah, you could eat it." and starts to laugh.

His friend says, "Is it moose cock?"

Q: How do you re-use a condom?
A: Turn it inside out and shake the fuck out of it.

After way to many drinks, a woman at a bar yells, "Hey, beefender, I need another martooni. I've got heartburn."

"First of all," the bartender says. "I'm a bartender and it's called a martini. Second of all, your tits are in the ashtray."

Sherlock Holmes and Dr Watson are in their study deep in thought when Holmes asks Watson to bend over and drop his pants. Always obedient, Watson drops his pants and bends over. When he does, Holmes shoves a lemon right up his ass.

"What the hell was that?" he cries.

"That my friend," Holmes says. "Was lemonentry.

It's Sunday and two priests are riding their bikes to church and as they see each other, they stop to chat for a couple of minutes before continuing on their separate ways.

The next Sunday, they see each other again, only this time one is walking and the other is riding his bike. The priest riding his bike sees the other walking and stops to see if everything is alright.

"I think one of my parishioners stole my bike." he says.

"I'll tell you what you do," the priest says. "During your sermon, recite the Ten Commandments and when you get to thou shall not steal, the person who took your bike will feel guilty and return it."

The priest says he'll do it and continues on his way to church.

The next Sunday, the priests see each other again and both have bikes. "I see my advice worked." Priest one says.

"Well, not exactly," priest two says. "I started to do as you said and when I got to thou shall not commit adultery, I remembered where I left my bike."

A bus full of ugly people crashes into an oncoming truck killing all of them. Feeling bad for them, God decides to grant them all one wish before letting them into Heaven.

"I want to be beautiful," says the hell pig at the front of the line. God snaps his fingers and she's beautiful.

The second person sees this and says, "I want to be beautiful too!" God snaps his fingers again and the wish is grated.

This goes on until God gets to the last guy in line that is rolling on the floor laughing. God, a little confused, asks the man for his wish.

"Make'em all ugly again!" he yells.

A Texan, New Yorker and a Bostonian are in a bar in the Yukon.

The Texan tosses back his shot, throws the half full bottle in the air, pulls out his gun and shoots the bottle blowing it apart. "Where I come from," he says. "We have plenty of liquor."

The New Yorker finishes his glass of wine, tosses the half full bottle in the air, pulls out his gun and blows it apart. "Where I come from," he says. "We have plenty of fine wine."

The guy from Boston finishes his beer to the last drop, tosses the empty bottle in the air, pulls out his gun and shoots the New Yorker right between the eyes. "Where I come from," he slowly says. "We never waste any booze and we got plenty of New Yorkers."

Q: What's the square root of 69?

A: Eight something.

A man, cheating on his not-so-bright girlfriend, keeps condoms in his wallet.

One day, she was going through his pants and finds the condoms and is not sure what they are so she asks him.

Quickly thinking, he tells her, "That's a condom, and it's to cover your cigarette in the rain so you can smoke. They sell them at the pharmacy."

Believing him, she goes to the pharmacy and asks the clerk for some condoms.

"No problem," the clerk says. "What size would you like?"

"Just big enough to fit a Camel." she tells him.

A blonde woman orders 20 gallons of milk to bathe in. The milkman, thinking it's a mistake, decides to ask her about it. "I'm sorry to trouble you ma'am," he says. "But are you sure you want 20 gallons of milk?"

"Absolutely," the blonde says. "I'm going to take a bath in it."

"Twenty it is then ma'am," the milkman says. "Pasteurized, right?"

"No, I don't think so," she says. "Probably just up to my nipples."

Q: How do you keep a kid from wetting the bed?

A: Give him an electric blanket.

A man drives his date up to lover's lane and parks.

"I have to be honest with you," his date says. "I'm a hooker and this night is going to cost you $25."

The man thinks about this for a minute then agrees to pay her $25 and they go at it.

After they finish, the man says, "Now, I have to be honest to. I'm really a cab driver and it's gonna cost you $25 to get back home."

Q: Why are married women fatter then single women?

A: Because single women open their refrigerator, see what they have and go to bed. Married women see who they have in bed then go to the refrigerator.

Two airplane mechanics, George and Ed, are working the same shift at the Philly airport in Philadelphia.

One night, there's a heavy fog and the two have nothing to do. Bored, George asks Ed, "Man, do you got anything to drink?"

"No," Ed says, "but, I hear you can get drunk off jet fuel."

So, the two drink the jet fuel, get drunk and have a good time.

The next morning, Ed calls George at home to see how he's feeling.

"I'm feeling fine." George says. "This is the best. We can drink all night with no hangovers."

"Well, there is one side effect," Ed tells him. "Have you farted yet?"

"No, why?" George asks him.

"I did," Ed says. "And I'm calling you from Arizona."

A seaman meets a pirate in a bar and they talk about their adventures. The seaman sees the pirate's peg-leg, hook and eye patch. "How did you end up with the peg leg?" he asks the pirate. "I was swept overboard into a school of sharks." the pirate says. "And as they were pulling me out, a shark bit off my leg."

"Incredible!" the seaman says. "And what about your hook?"

"Well," the pirate replies. "We were invading a ship when one of the enemy cut off my hand."

"Amazing!" the seaman says. "How did you get the eye patch?"

"A sea gull shit in my eye," the pirate tells him.

"You lost your eye to sea gull shit?" he asks the pirate.

"Well," the pirate says. "It was my first day with the hook."

An elephant tells a camel, "It sure is funny that you have tits on your back."

The camel just laughs and says, "Ain't that some shit coming from someone with a dick on his face!"

A man gets invited back to a woman's house who works for the carnival. After a little foreplay, they get down to business. The guy finishes and sees that the woman has a lot of stuffed animals. Feeling confident, he asks her, "So, how was I?"

Calmly, the woman replies, "Take something from the bottom shelf."

Hung Chow calls into work and tells his boss, "Hey, I No come to work today, I sick, headache, stomachache, I no come to work."

His boss tells him, "You know something Hung Chow, I really need you today. When I feel like that, I go to my wife and tell her to give me sex. That makes me better and I go to work. You try it."

Three hours later, Hung Chow calls his boss and says, "I do what you say, I feel great. I be work soon. You got nice house."

Q: What should a woman say to a man she's just had sex with?

A: Whatever she wants. He's sleeping.

"Bartender!" a young man yells as he enters the bar. "Line me up six shots of vodka!"

The bartender lines up the six shots and the young man downs them all back-to-back.

"Wow," the bartender says. "What's the occasion?"

"My first blowjob." the young man tells him.

"Well then, the seventh shot is on the house." the bartender tells him.

"No thanks," the young man says. "If the first six won't get the taste out off my mouth, nothing will."

One day, Kevin comes home from the pickle factory where he works and tells his wife that he has a terrible urge to stick his penis into the pickle slicer. His wife suggest that he see a sex therapist to talk about it, but Kevin says he'd be too embarrassed and promises to overcome the urge on his own. A couple of weeks later, Kevin comes home ashen.

"What's wrong, dear?" his wife asks.

"Do you remember that I told you I had the urge to stick my penis in the pickle slicer?"

"Oh, Kevin, please tell me you didn't."

"Yeah, I did."

"My God, What happened?"

"She and I got fired."

Mad about having to do his farm duties before breakfast, a little boy stomps outside to feed the animals. When he gets over to the chickens, he kicks one of them across the yard. He goes to feed one of the cows and kicks the cow, too. After that, he kicks a pig. Back inside, his mother gives him a bowl of dry cereal.

"How come I don't have any milk in my cereal?" he asks his mom. "And why don't I have any eggs or bacon?"

"Well," his mother says. "I saw you kick that chicken, so no eggs for a week. I also saw you kick the pig, so no bacon for a week. And, I saw you kick the cow so, no milk either for a week."

At that moment, his father comes in for breakfast and kicks the cat half way across the kitchen. The boy looks at his mother with a smile on his face and says, "So, are you gonna tell him or should I?"

Q: How did Steve Wonder feel about the cheese grater he got for Christmas?

A: He thought it was the most violent book he's ever read.

Q: What's the difference between sex for money and sex for free?

A: Sex for money usually costs less.

A man walks into a bar and orders a triple scotch. As the bartender pours the drink, he remarks, "That's a pretty stiff drink, everything ok?"

After downing his drink, the man says, "I just found my wife in bed with my best friend."

"What'd you do?" the bartender asked him.

"I walked right over to my wife, looked her right in the eye and told her to pack her shit and get the hell out."

"Good move," the bartender says. "And what about your best friend?"

"I walked over to him, looked him right in the eye and yelled 'Bad dog!'"

A man walked into his local library and asked the librarian for a book on Tourette 's syndrome. The librarian says, "Fuck off, asshole!"

"Yep," the man says. "That's the one."

Two guys walking down the street come across a sheep with its head stuck in a fence. One of them says, "I'm kinda horny," then starts to have sex with the sheep.

When he's done, he turns to his friend and asks him, "Do you want to take a turn?"

"Sure!" the friend says.

His horny friend then drops his pants and sticks his head in the fence and says, "Ok, I'm ready!"

Q: Why do they call it the wonder bra?

A: Because when a woman takes it off, you wonder where her tits went.

A man applies to be a truck driver at a new trucking company and gets hired.

"I've got one demand though," the man tells his new employer. "Since you hired me, you got to hire Ryan."

"Who's that?" his new boss asks him.

"He's my partner. He drives when I sleep and I drive when he sleeps." the new guy says. "You got to take Ryan."

"Well, if you can answer this question to my satisfaction, I'll hire Ryan, too." the boss says. "You're going down a hill and your brakes go out. Up ahead is a bridge with an 18-wheeler jack-knifed across it. What do you do?"

"I'd wake up Ryan." the new guy says.

"How's that gonna help you?"

"Well, we've been together for 30 years," the new guy says, "and he ain't never seen a wreck like the one were about to have!"

A guy walks into a bar and asks the bartender for a beer. "Yes sir, that will be one cent." the bartender says.

"One cent!" the man marvels. "That's awesome!" Then, he looks at the menu and orders the best steak.

"Yes sir that will cost you four cents." the bartender says.

"Four cents!" the man says surprised. "Where's the guy who owns this place?"

"He's upstairs with my wife." the bartender tells him.

"What's he doing with your wife?" the man asks him.

"The same thing I'm doing to his business." the bartender tells him.

A man walks into his bedroom where his wife is laying in bed.

He's got two aspirins and a glass of water.
"What's that for?" his wife asks him.
"It's for your headache," he replies.
"But I don't have a headache," she says.
"Gotcha!" her husband says.

Q: How are blowjobs like Eggs Benedict?

A: They're both something you'll never get at home.

A man comes home from work one day to find his wife on the porch with two suitcases beside her.

"Where are you going?" he asks.

"I'm moving out to Las Vegas," she tells him. "I found out that I can charge $400 a night for what I give you for free."

The guy runs inside and comes back out with his bags packed, too. "I'm going to!" he tells her.

"Why?" she asks.

"Well," he says. "I want to see how you're gonna live on $800 a year."

A man sitting on a park bench is watching two city workers work.

Both of them have shovels and as the one digs a hole, the second worker comes along and fills it in. The man sits there for an hour and watches them work like this. Finally, the man can take no more and walks up to the men and says, "I appreciate how hard you guys are working, but what the hell are you really doing? One of you digs a hole and then the other just fills it back in."

"Well," the hole digger says. "The guy who plants the trees is sick today."

Q: You have two minutes to live. What's the best kind of candy to eat?

A: A lifesaver.

A tour bus is stopped in the middle of town in Egypt and all the passengers get off to go shopping in the town square.

About an hour later, one of the tourist asks a local man what time it is. The local, who's sitting next to his camel reaches over and softly lifts the camel's balls in his hand and lifts them up and down. "It's about 4:30." he says.

Amazed, the tourist runs back to the bus to confirm that its 4:30. "The man sitting over there by the camel can tell time by the weight of a camels balls!" He tells the rest of the tourist. Not belicving this, another tourist goes over and asks the local what time it is. The local again, lifts the camel's balls and gets the time right. The tourist runs back to the bus to confirm the others story.

Finally, the bus driver goes over and asks the local man how he can tell the time just by lifting a camels balls.

"Sit down and grab the camel's balls," the local tells the bus driver. "Now lift them up so you can see the clock on the other side of the courtyard."

Q: What's the best thing about dating a homeless girl?

A: When the date ends, you can drop her off anywhere.

A couple takes their young son to the circus. When his father goes to get some snacks, the boy asks his mom, "Mom, what's that long thing on the elephant?"

"That's the elephant's trunk," his mom tells him.

"No, mom, underneath the elephant."

Blushing, his mother says, "Oh, that's nothing."

The boy's father comes back and his mother gets up to use the bathroom. As soon as she leaves, the boy asks his father the same question.

"That's the elephant's trunk, son." his dad says.

"I know what an elephant's trunk is, dad. The thing down there."

"That's just his penis," his father tells him.

"How come when I asked mom what it was she said it was nothing," the boy asks his father.

His father takes a deep breath and says, "Son, I've spoiled that woman."

A man with no arms or legs is on the beach sunbathing when he is approached by three beautiful women who take pity on him.

The first asks him, "Have you ever been hugged?" The man shakes his head no and she bends down and gives him a hug.

The second woman asks him, "Have you ever been kissed?" He shakes his head no and she bends down to give him a kiss.

The third woman then asks him, "Have you ever been fucked?" "No," says the man, his eye lighting up.

"Well, you're about to be, the tides coming in."

It's poker night at Bill's house and unfortunately, his wife works nights and he's stuck watching little Billy. The kid is a mess. During the game, he's knocking over beers, throwing chips and yelling out everyone's cards. Bill's buddies are getting pissed, but every time he chases Billy out of the room, he comes back in screaming even louder. Finally, Bill takes the kid and drags him to the bathroom. He comes back to the table a while later and they continue to play cards. A couple of hours go by before someone asks what happened to the kid.

"Yeah, Bill," a friend says, "What'd you do, kill him?"

"Hell no," Bill says. "I taught the little bastard how to jerk off."

Q: What's Snoop Dogg's favorite kind of weather?

A: Drizzle.

Visiting a psych ward one day, a man asks the doctors how they decide to commit a patient.

"Well," the director says. "We fill a bath tub with water and then offer a teaspoon, a teacup or a bucket to the patient and tell them to empty the tub."

"I get it," the visitor says. "A normal person would use the bucket because it's the biggest."

"No,' the director says. "A normal person would pull the stopper."

One day in the locker room, Ned sees a fat man with a cork in his

ass. He asks the man why he's got it there.

"Well," the man says. "I was walking down the street one day and kicked this lamp. There was a puff of smoke and a big genie in a turban came out and said, 'I'm a genie and will grant you one wish.' I said 'No shit!'"

A vampire bat goes back to his cave covered in blood. The other bats hound him until he takes them to the source of the blood. After leading the pack for more than a mile, the first bat slows down and says, "See that oak tree over there?"

"Yes, yes!" all the other bats scream.

"That's interesting," the first bat says. "Because I fucking didn't."

An agent discovers that his top client had been moonlighting as an

escort. Having lusted after her for years, he asks if he can have sex with her, too. She agrees, but tells him, "You'll have to pay the same as everyone else."

The agent thinks this is unfair, but agrees to it and the two go back to her house. He turns out the lights and they have sex. She falls asleep, but ten minutes later, she's awakened and the scene repeats itself. It goes on like this for ten hours.

The actress is amazed at her agent's stamina. "I never knew agents were so virile." she tells him.

"Lady, I'm not your agent." her lover says. "He's at the front door selling tickets."

Q: Why did the chicken go across the basketball court?

A: He heard the ref was blowing fowls.

"I'm sorry Dan, but you don't have more than a month to live." the doctor says.

Dan is dismayed. "But Doctor," Dan says. "This is the best I've felt in years. It just can't be true. Is there anything I can do?"

"I'll tell you what you do," the doctor tells him. "Go to a health spa and start taking a mud bath every day."

Agreeing, Dan asks the doctor, "Will that help me?"

"No, but it will get you used to the dirt." the doctor says.

A woman is looking for an exotic pet at her local pet store when she sees a box labeled "Sex Frogs-$20 each! Satisfaction guaranteed"

The woman tells the pet shop employee she'd like to buy one of the frogs.

"Just follow the instructions on the box. If you have any questions, please call the store."

When the woman gets home, she starts to follow the instructions on the box:

1) take a shower,

2) put on sexy lingerie,

3) put on romantic music,

4) get into bed with the frog.

Nothing happens and the woman calls the store frustrated.

"I'll be right over," the clerk tells her.

When the clerk gets there, the woman says, "I followed the instructions to the letter, but the frog just sits there."

The clerk picks up the frog and says, "Listen to me! I'm only going to show you how to do this one more time."

The rabbi and the priest meet at the town's annual picnic. Being old friends, they start their usual banter.

"This ham is really delicious," the priest teased the rabbi. "You really have to try it. I know it's against your religion, but you just haven't lived until you've tried Mrs. Hall's Virginia baked ham. When are you going to break down and have a slice?"

The rabbi looked at his friend with a big smile and said, "At your wedding."

Q: Did you ever date a midget?

A: Yeah, I was just nuts over her.

One weekend, a doctor a priest and a lawyer were out in a fishing boat.

Their motor dies and one of the oars drifts off. Just as the doctor was about to jump in to get the oar, their boat was surrounded by sharks.

"I can't go in now," the doctor says. "If someone gets bitten, they'll need my services."

"I can't go in either," the priest says. "If someone dies, I'll need to give the last rights."

"Fine, I'll get it." the attorney says. He dives in and the sharks move. He gets the oar back and gets back in the boat. The doctor and priest look flabbergasted.

The attorney just smiles and says, "Professional courtesy."

President Hussein calls President Clinton at the White House and tells him, "Bill, I had the most amazing dream last night. I could see the whole America and on each house there was a banner on it."

Clinton asks him, "Well, Saddam, what was on the banners?"

Hussein says, "Allah is God, God is Allah."

Clinton says, "I'm glad you called Saddam, I too had a dream last night and could see all of Baghdad and it was as beautiful as ever. It was completely rebuilt and each house also had a banner on it."

Hussein asks him, "What did you see on the banners?"

Clinton says, "I don't know. I can't read Hebrew."

One night, a man storms into his bedroom with a sheep under his arm and stands in front of his wife. "This is the pig I have to screw when you have a headache." he says.

His wife looks up at him and says, "That's a sheep under your arm."

"Shut up, I wasn't talking to you."

A prostitute is brought before a judge for solicitation. She pleads not guilty. "I am celibate." she tells the judge.

"Celibate?" the judge asks her. "How can you claim to be celibate?"

"It's my business to be celibate," she says. "I sell a bit here, I sell a bit there."

The president of a company gets together all the employees of his company. "Someone here has been spreading a rumor that I'm in the KKK." the boss says. "Who made this rumor up?"

There's a long silence before his secretary raises her hand and says, "There's been a misunderstanding. I never said you were in the KKK, I just told some of the girls you were a wizard under the sheets."

Q: How do you find the blind man in a nudist colony?

A: It's not hard.

A man and woman are on the train to Philly in the first class

section. The man would sneeze, then pull out his penis and wipe off the tip. The woman can't believe what she is seeing.

After a couple of minutes more, the man sneezes again. Again, he pulls out his penis and wipes off the tip. The woman is about to go crazy. She can't believe someone so rude would exist. After it happens for a third time, she turns to the man and says, "What the hell is wrong with you, you sick bastard?"

"I'm sorry, ma'am," the man says. "I have a rare condition that whenever I sneeze, I have an orgasm."

"I'm sorry," the woman says. "But you have to admit that's very strange. What do you take for it?"

"Pepper." the man tells her.

A man goes to his doctor for a checkup.

Afterwards, the doctor comes out and tells him, "I'm afraid I have some really bad news for you. You're dying and don't have much time left."

"My God!" the man says. "How much time do I got left?"

"Ten," the doctor says.

"Ten?" the man asks. "Ten what? Months? Weeks? What?"

The doctor interrupts him, "Nine..."

An artist asks a gallery owner if there has been any interest in any of his paintings that the owner is displaying.

"I've got some good news and I've got some bad news for you." the owner tells him. "The good news is that a man asked about your work and asked if your paintings would appreciate in value after your death. When I told him it would, he bought all of your paintings."

"That's great!" the artist says. "So, what's the bad news?"

"The guy was your doctor." the owner tells him.

Q: What has four legs and one arm?

A: A happy Rottweiler.

A bunch of boys are fishing at their favorite spot when the game warden pulls up and jumps out of his truck. One boy throws down his fishing pole and takes off running through the woods with the warden giving chase. After running almost a mile, the boy stops and the game warden catches him.

"Let me see your fishing license boy!" the game warden yells to him.

The boy pulls out his license and shows it to the game warden.

"Boy," says the game warden. "You are dumber then a box of rocks. You don't have to run from me. You got a valid license."

"I know I do," the boy says. "But the other guy back there didn't."

Q: What's the safest speed for having sex?

A: 68, because at 69 you flip over and eat it.

A hunter spots a small brown bear in the woods and shoots it. All

of a sudden, he feels a tap on his shoulder. He turns and is face-to-face with a big brown bear.

"You've got two choices," the bear says. "We have sex or I maul you."

The hunter decides to take it from the bear. After recovering for three weeks, the pissed off hunter searches out and shoots the big brown bear. Just then he fells a tap on his shoulder and turns to see a 10-foot grizzly standing there.

"Admit it," the bear says. "You don't come here for the hunting, do you?"

A desperate man is about to have sex with a terribly obese woman and climbs on top of her.

"Do you mind if I turn the ceiling light off?" he asks her.

"Why?" the beast asks. "Are you shy?"

"Not at all," the man says. "It's just that the light is burning my ass."

A prostitute finishes her work for the night and calls a taxi. When it pulls to her stop, the driver asks for his fare. "Please sir," the prostitute says. "I just realized I forgot my purse."

"Then how do you intend to pay for this fare?" the driver asks her.

The prostitute lifts up her skirt.

"Got anything smaller?" he asks her.

Little boy writes to Santa, "Could you please send me a little sister."

Santa writes him back, "Please send me your mother."

Q: How is a soy burger like a dildo?

A: They are both substitutes for meat.

A little old lady walks into a biker bar and finds the dirtiest, meanest looking biker in the place and says, "Young man, I want to ride with your gang."

"You can't ride with us, old lady," the guy says. "Where's your bike?"

The old lady points to a Harley parked outside and says, "That's my chopper right out there."

"That's a nice bike," the biker tells her. "But we're some mean bastards. You ain't mean enough to ride with us."

Before he can react, the old lady clocks the guy behind her with her purse, whacks him in the face with her cane, then kicks him in the balls and the man goes down.

"Ok," the biker says. "That's pretty mean. But have you ever been picked up by the fuzz?"

"No," the old lady says. "But I have been swung around by my titties a couple of times."

A man goes to his doctor for his annual checkup. After his check up, his doctor tells him, "I've got some good news and some bad news."

"Give me the good news first, doc" the man says.

"The good news is that your penis is going to be two inches longer and an inch wider." the doctor tells him.

"That's fantastic!" the patient says. "So, what's the bad news?"

"It's malignant."

If you were gas in my ass I would never fart for fear of losing you, cuz you're the shit!

A guy out on a date tries to impress his date with his knowledge of fine wines. He tells the wine steward to bring him a bottle of 1985 Sterling Cabernet from the Carneros district. After the man taste the wine he tells the steward, "This is a 1990 vintage from the Diamond Creek vineyard in Martha's vineyard. Please bring me what I ordered."

An old drunk watching from the bar comes up to the man with a glass in his hand and says, "Can you tell me what this is?"

Winking at his date, the man takes a sip from the drunk's glass. Spitting it out, he says, "This taste like fucking piss!"

"It is," the drunk says. "But what year?"

Mark and Chad are two old guys who walk in the park and talk baseball every day. One day, Mark asks, "Chad, do you think there's baseball in Heaven?"

"I don't have a clue, Mark," Chad says. "But, let's make a deal.

Whichever one of us dies first, we have to come back and let the other know if there is."

They shake on it. A few months later, Mark dies. One day a couple of weeks later, Chad is walking in the park alone when he hears a voice say his name.

"Mark, is that you?" Chad asks.

"Yeah, Chad." Mark's ghost whispers.

"So, is there baseball in heaven?" Chad asks his ghost.

"Well," Mark's ghost says. "I got some good news and some bad news."

"I want the good news first!" Chad says.

"Well, there is baseball in Heaven." Mark says.

"That's wonderful," Chad says. "What's the bad news then?"

"The bad news is," Mark says sadly. "You're pitching on Friday."

A hiker lost in the woods spends three days wondering around with no food. He finally spots a bald eagle on a tree limb and kills it with a big rock and starts to eat it. A park ranger comes across him as he's eating it and arrests him for killing an endangered species.

While in court, the man tells the judge he had no choice because he was about to starve to death.

"Given the circumstances, I find you not guilty," the judge says. "But I do have to ask you, what did it taste like?"

"Well, it sort of tasted like a cross between a whooping crane and a spotted owl.'

The residents of a small town keep falling down a deep sink hole in the middle of town on the sidewalk on Main Street and always end up dying because the closest hospital is over 50 miles away. The mayor calls a town meeting to discuss the issue and asks for any suggestions.

"We need to get our own hospital," one of the locals say.

"We can' afford that," the mayor says. "Anything else?"

"I got the perfect idea," a redneck says. "Let's just dig the hole next to the hospital."

Father Sam wakes up to a beautiful, sunny Sunday morning and decides he wants to play golf instead of saying mass. He calls an associate pastor and tells him he's sick and asks him if he can do his mass for him. The associate pastor says he will and Father Sam goes 50 miles out of town to play golf so he won't be seen by anyone from his parish. He gets there only to discover he has the whole course to himself because everyone else is in church. Watching all this from the Heavens, St. Peter asks the Lord, "Are you going to let him get away with this?"

At that moment, Father Sam hits the ball and it goes straight for the pin, dropping a little short of it then rolls up and drops in the hole. It's a 490 yard hole in one.

Confused, St. Peter looks at the Lord and asks Him, "Why in the world would, you let him do that?"

The Lord smiles and says, "Who's he going to tell?"

Two mailmen are taking on the sidewalk after finishing their routes for the day when one of them stomps on a slug.

"Why'd you do that?" the other mailman asks him.

"The first mailman wipes his shoe off and says, "That bastards been following me all day."

A beautiful woman goes to the gynecologist. The doctor sees her and all of his professionalism leaves his mind. He immediately tells her to undress. Once naked, the doctor begins stroking her thigh.

"Do you know what I'm doing?" he asks her.

"You're checking for any abrasions or abnormalities," she says.

"That's correct," the doctor says as he begins to fondle her breasts. "Do you know what I'm doing now?"

"You're checking for lumps for breast cancer." the woman says.

"That's right," the doctor says. Deciding to go for it all, he mounts her and starts to have sex with her. "Do you know what I'm doing now?"

"Yes," she says. "You're getting herpes, which is what I came here for in the first place."

A man comes in front of St. Peter at the pearly gates. "Have you done anything of particular merit?" St. Peter asks the man.

"I came across a bunch of bikers harassing a woman and her child in a parking lot," the man says. "I told the bikers to leave them alone. The bikers wouldn't listen, so I went up to the meanest looking one, smacked him on the head, kicked his bike over and threw him to the ground and told him to back the hell off."

Impressed, St. Peter asked the man, "When did this happen?"

"Oh, about five minutes ago." the man answers.

Two guys are hiking up a mountain when they come across a crowd of people bungee jumping. One says to the other, "Want to give it a try?"

"Hell no," the other says. "I came into this world because of a broken rubber. I'm not leaving it the same way."

A cowboy and his new bride check into a motel for their honeymoon. The cowboy tells the clerk that they were just married that morning.

"Would you like the bridal?" the clerk asks him.

"No thanks," the cowboy says. "I'll just hold her by the ears till she gets the hang of it."

Marcus is at the urinal in the restroom when a guy with no arms comes up next to him and says, "Hey, buddy, can you help me out here?"

Feeling uncomfortable, Marcus unzips the man's zipper, takes a deep breath and reaches in and pulls the guy's penis out. Marcus is horrified. The man's penis in hideous. It's moldy and bluish green and covered with puss filled scabs and smells awful. Marcus still holds the man's penis until the man finishes, puts it back and zips him up.

The guy tells Marcus, "Thanks, buddy."

"Not a problem," Marcus says. "But what the hell is wrong with your Johnson?"

Poking his arms out of his sleeves, the guy says, "I don't know, but I sure as hell ain't touching it."

"Knock, knock."

"Who's there?"

"Control freak.

Now, this is where you say 'control freak who?'"

A rich man and his wife are served dinner by their personal chef.

"You know," the husband says to his wife. "If you learned to cook, we could save a ton of money."

"True, dear," his wife says. "And if you learned to screw, we could fire the pool boy, too."

Three old men are sitting around the old folks home complaining.

"I wish I could take a leak without the pain," the first old man says.

"Quit your bitching," the second old man says. "I'm so constipated, I can't have a regular bowel movement."

"That's nothing," the third old man says. "I have a nice long pee at 6:30 and then I have a bowel movement at 7:00."

"Then what the hell are you complaining about?" the first man asks.

"I don't wake up till 7:30," the third man tells him.

A man goes up to a street vendor and orders a hot dog.

The vendor grabs the hot dog with his bare hands and puts it on the bun. Then he applies the relish with his fingers.

The customer pulls out a badge and says, "I'm with the health department and I'm shutting you down!"

The vendor pleads with the inspector and promises to clean up his act. The inspector agrees, but tells him he will be stopping back by, unannounced.

A couple of weeks later, the inspector stops back and orders a hot dog with relish again. The vendor uses tongs and grabs the hot dog and uses another pair to put the relish on.

"You've passed," the inspector tells the vendor before noticing a string hanging out of his zipper. "Wait, what's that string for?" The vendor says, "I'm so clean that when I go to the bathroom, I don't even touch myself."

"Then how do you get it back in your pants?" the inspector asks him.

"I use the tongs."

Three men are in a bar drinking when a old drunk stumbles in, comes up to them and points to the guy in the middle and says, "Your mom is the best lay in town!"

Everyone expects a fight, but the man ignores the drunk and goes to the other end of the bar. Five minutes later, the drunk goes back up to the man and says, "I just screwed your mom and it was sweet!"

Again, the man ignores the drunk and wanders off to the other side of the bar.

After another five minutes, the drunk comes up to the guy again and says, "Your mom even let me."

Finally, the man says, "Go home dad, your drunk!"

A Texas oil tycoon storms into his lawyer's office and tells him that he wants him to start divorce proceedings against his wife. "I want to sue that adulterous bitch for breach of contract," he tells his lawyer.

"I don't know if we'll have a case," his lawyer tells him. "Your wife isn't a piece of property. You don't own her."

"Maybe you right," the oil tycoon says. "But I sure as hell should have exclusive drilling rights."

On their wedding night, a bride demands that her husband give her $25 for their first sexual encounter. In his highly aroused state of mind, he agrees. For the next 35 years, she demanded $25 every time they made love. Her husband always agreed, thinking it was her way to get clothes and jewelry. One day she came home to find her husband distraught.

"I've been fired," her husband says. "I have no money and we'll probably have to live on the street."

"I don't think so," she says. "The office building where you worked is yours. The apartment building down the street is yours, too. I took the money you gave me for sex and invested it every month."

Her husband becomes even more upset.

"What's wrong?' she asked him. "I thought you'd be happy."

"If I'd have known that's what you were doing, I would have given you all my business." her husband says.

A mother is concerned because her 9 year old son has never spoken a word in his life. One day while eating lunch he looks up and says, "My soups cold."

Amazed, his mother asks him, "I've waited so long for you to speak. Why have you waited till now?"

The boy shrugs and says, "Up till now, everything's been fine."

A new nun goes to her first confession at her new church. She tells the priest that she has a terrible secret she needs to confess.

The priest tells her that her secret is safe with the church.

She says, "Father, I never wear any panties under my habit."

The priest smiles to himself and tells her, "That's not so serious, sister. Just do five Hail Mary's, five Our Fathers and five cartwheels."

Two four year old boys are standing at the toilet to pee. One says to the other, "Wow! What the hell is up with your ding-dong?"

"I was circumcised," the boy says. "They cut the skin off when I was three days old."

"Did it hurt?" asks the first boy.

"Did it hurt?!?" the second boy says. "I didn't walk for a year!"

An old man is eating at a truck stop when three Hells Angels walk in.

The first Hells Angel walks up to the old man, puts his cigarette out in his pie then sits at the counter.

The second Hells Angel walks up, spits in the old man's coffee and also sits at the counter.

The third Hells Angel walks up, flips the old man's plate over and he sits at the counter with the other two.

Without a word, the old man gets up and leaves.

"He's not much of a man, is he?" one of them asks the waitress.

"He's not much of a truck driver either," the waitress says. "He just backed over three motorcycles outside."

On the first day of kindergarten, the teacher asks each student to count to 60.

Some do it as high as 40 or 50 and others can't get past 20.

Robby counts up to 100 with no problem.

He gets home and tells his dad how good he did and his dad says, "That's because you're from Alabama, son."

The next day, the teacher tells the students to say the alphabet. Most only make it half way through, but Robby says it with no problems.

When he gets home and tells his dad how good he did, his dad simply says, "That's because you're from Alabama, son."

The next day, after gym class, the boys are taking showers and Robby sees that his penis is bigger than anyone else's. That night he tells his dad, "Dad, mines bigger than anyone else's in class. Is that because I'm from Alabama?"

"No," his dad says. "That's because your 25."

A turtle is walking down the street in New York when he's mugged by a gang of snails.

A police detective comes to find out what happened and asks the turtle what happened.

The turtle, a little confused says, "I don't know, it all happened so fast."

Q: How many rednecks does it take to eat a possum?

A: Three. One to eat it and two to watch for cars.

A newly married sailor was informed by the navy that he will be stationed overseas for two

years. A few weeks after getting there, he starts to really miss his wife and writes her a letter. "My darling, it looks like we will be apart for a long time. I already miss you and we are always surrounded by beautiful women. The temptation is killing me. I need a hobby to keep my mind off of them."

His wife sends him back a flute with a note that says, "Why don't you learn to play this?"

After the two years is up, he rushes back to his wife. "Baby," he says to her. "I can't wait to get you into bed to make love to you!"

She stops him with a wave of his hand. "First, let me see how good you play that flute I sent you."

Three smiling corpses are lying in a morgue and the local detective arrives to determine the cause of death and why they're smiling.

The corner points to the first corpse and says, "This is Jed, he died after winning the million dollar lottery."

He goes to the second smiling corpse and says, "This is Tom-Tom, he died in the middle of having sex with his neighbor."

Then, he then come to the third smiling corpse and says, "This is Bob, he died after being hit by lightning."

"What the hell was he smiling for then?" the detective asked. "He thought he was getting his picture taken." the corner says.

Pinocchio and his girlfriend are in bed having sex when she sighs.

He asks her why and she says, "You're the best lover I ever had, but every time we have sex, you give me splinters."

This really bothers him so, the next day he asks Gepetto for some advice.

He suggests some sandpaper to 'smooth out' his relationship with his girlfriend. Pinocchio thanks his creator and goes on his way.

A couple of weeks later, Gepetto sees Pinocchio at the hardware store buying every packet of sandpaper in stock.

"I guess things are going better between you and your girlfriend now, huh?" Gepetto says.

"Girlfriend?" Pinocchio says. "Who needs a girlfriend?"

A captain in the Foreign Legion was transferred to the desert

outpost. Once there, he notices an old, seedy looking camel tied up behind the barracks. He asks his sergeant what the camel was for.

The sergeant tells him, "Well sir, we're a far distance from the nearest town and the men have urges. So, when they do, we have the camel."

The captain says, "Well, if it's good for morale, I suppose its ok then."

After being there for about six months, the captain could hardly control his own urges and could stand it no longer and goes looking for the sergeant.

"Bring me the camel," he said.

The sergeant just shrugs and leads the camel into his quarters where the captain hops onto a stool and starts to have vigorous sex with the camel. As he steps down, satisfied, doing up his pants, he asks the sergeant "Is that how the enlisted men do it?"

"Well, no sir," the sergeant says. "They usually just ride it in town to the brothel."

While making love for the first time, Aaron sees that his girl friend's toes are curling with each of his thrust. Thrust, curl, thrust, curl. I am one serious lover he thinks.

Later when he's making love to her in the shower, he sees that he's unable to yet the same reaction. After brooding for a couple of minutes, he gets up the courage to ask his girlfriend why she's not as excited.

"Well, I am," she tells him. "It's just that now I'm not wearing any pantyhose."

A man from Colorado has 20 wives whom he makes love to every day. A Las Vegas promoter hears of the man's daily routine and hires him to show off his prowess.

On opening night, the man is only able to make love to 10 of his wives before collapsing in exhaustion.

Once the curtain falls, the promoter runs up to the man and asks him, "What happened?"

"I don't know," the man says. "Everything went fine today at practice."

Q: Why do men in Scotland wear kilts?

A: Because sheep can hear the zipper a mile away.

A man is playing golf with his wife when, teeing off at the sixth hole, his ball lands on a branch in a cluster of trees. He's about to take a drop when his wife points out an easier way to scale the tree and take the shot.

The husband does so and whacks the ball. It ricochets off another branch and hits his wife in the head, killing her instantly.

Months later, the man is playing the same hole with a friend. He drives the ball, it lands in the same branch and he opts to take the drop.

"Don't do that," his friend says. "You can climb the tree and play on."

"God no," the man says. "I tried that once before and it was a total disaster. I scored a nine."

A fat guy sees a sign that reads "Lose weight. $10 a pound. Call (555) 555-4301" and decides to make the call.

The operator asks him," How much weight do you want to lose?"

"About ten pounds," he tells her.

"We'll have someone over in the morning." she tells him.

Around 10:00 a.m. there's a knock on the door. Standing there is a fairly good-looking girl completely naked except for the sign around her neck that reads, "If you can catch me, you can have sex with me."

The fat guy chases her upstairs, downstairs, and all over the house. After catching her, they have sex and then he runs to the bathroom to weigh himself and he's lost ten pounds.

Later that night, he calls the number again and says, "I want to lose 20 pounds!"

"We'll send someone over in the morning," the operator tells him. The next morning, he answers his door to find a beautiful woman wearing nothing but some track shoes and a sign that says, "If you catch me, you can have sex with me."

The fat guy takes off after her and after a little while longer this time, he finally catches her. They have sex and when he weighs himself; he's lost another 20 pounds.

That night, he calls the number again and says, "I want to lose 50 pounds!"

"Fifty pounds?" the operator asks him. That's a lot of weight to lose."

"Just take care of it," the man tells her.

About 8:00 the next morning, the fat man opens his door to find an enormous gorilla with a sign around his neck that says, "It I catch you..."

Strolling through the park, Sherlock Holmes and Dr. Watson pass three women sitting on a bench eating bananas.

"Good day, ladies." Sherlock says.

"Do you know them, sir?" Holmes asks him.

"If you are referring to the nun, the whore and the married woman, no I don't." Sherlock tells him.

"How did you deduce that, sir?"

"Easily, my dear friend." Sherlock says. "The nun eats her banana in small slices and the whore shoves it down her throat with both hands."

"Was the third wearing a wedding ring?" Watson asks.

"No, she was holding the banana with one hand and shoving her head toward it with the other."

Q: What was the first commandment?

A: Adam, pull out.

A wife wakes up in the middle of the night one night to find her husband missing from bed. After checking the house, she hears sounds coming from the basement. She goes downstairs and finds her husband down there crying.

"Honey, what's wrong?" she ask him really worried about him and wondering what could make a man cry like that.

"Remember 20 years ago when I got you pregnant and your father threatened me to marry you or go to prison?"

"Of course I do." she said.

"I would have been released tonight."

Shortly after a couple is married they have a baby. Sadly, the baby is born without any arms, legs or even a torso. Even though their child is just a head, they dedicate their lives to raising and loving him.

After twenty years, the couple takes a much needed vacation. On vacation, they meet a doctor who's achieved a medical breakthrough. "I know how to make your child whole again," the Doctor says.

The couple runs home to their bodiless child and tells him the great news.

"Honey!" the mom says. "We're back from our vacation and have a surprise for you!"

"Oh, no," the head says. "Not another fucking hat!"

A lawyer parks his brand new Jaguar and just as he steps out, a truck comes barreling down the street and tears the driver's side door off.

The lawyer calls 911 and within minutes, the police arrive. But before he says anything, the lawyer starts screaming about how his new Jaguar is wrecked beyond repair.

When the lawyer calms down, the cop shakes his head in disgust. "I can't believe how materialistic you lawyers are," he says. "You're so focused on your possessions, that you don't notice anything else."

"How the hell can you say such a thing?" the lawyer asks.

"Your left arm is torn off from the elbow down," the cop tells him. "It must have been torn off in the accident."

"My God!" the lawyer says. "Where's my Rolex?"

Rick goes to a diner and orders the special - chili.

"The man next to you got the last bowl," the waitress says. "Want something else?"

"Let me just have a coffee then," Rick says.

After a couple of minutes, Rick sees that the guy is done and that his chili bowl is still full.

"Are you going to eat that?" he asks the man.

"Nope, you can have it if you want."

Rick grabs his bowl and is half way done when he finds a dead mouse in the chili and pukes in the bowl.

The man just looks up and says, "That's about as far as I got before I threw up."

Late one Saturday night a drunk checks into a hotel. When he finally wakes up, he has the worst hangover of his life and immediately calls down to the desk for a bottle of whiskey and the Sunday paper. After six hours, the bellhop arrives with the man's order.

"It took you long enough," the man says. "It must be impossible to buy a bottle in this town on Sunday."

"The liquor wasn't the problem sir," the bellhop says. "But it's a bitch finding a Sunday paper on Tuesday."

A man goes into a bar and orders 10 shots of tequila.

The bartender looks at the guy as he downs one after the other.

As he slams the 8th one, the bartender says, I don't think you should be drinking those so fast."

"You'd drink them this fast if you had what I have." the man says throwing back number 9.

"And what is it that you have?" the bartender asks him.

The man throws back his last shot and says, "One dollar."

A young punk gets on the bus and sits directly across from an old man. The kid has green, orange and yellow hair and his clothes are tattered and his earrings have big red, blue and green feathers on them.

The old man can't help but stare.

After a while, the punk says, "What are you starring at? Didn't you ever do anything wild when you were young?"

"Sure, I did," the old man says. "Back when I was in the navy, I got drunk and screwed a parrot in Singapore. I thought you might be my son."

Three couples, one retired, one middle-aged and one newlywed, visit a minister and ask to join his church.

The minister tells them that they first must go two weeks without sex and come back and tell him how it went.

The two weeks pass and all three couples return to church.

The older couple said they had no problem abstaining.

The middle-aged couple said it was hard for the first week, but that they were fine after that.

The newlyweds say it was fine until the wife dropped a can of paint.

"A can of paint?" the minister asks.

"Yeah, paint," the husband says. "She dropped the can and when she bent over to pick it up, I had to have her right then and there."

The minister just shakes his head and tells them they're not welcome in his church.

"That's ok," the man says. "We're not welcome in Home Depot either."

A man asks the only other man in the bar if he can buy him a drink.

"Of course you can," the man says.

The first man then asks him, "Where are you from?"

"Ireland," the second man says.

"I'm from Ireland, too. Let's have another drink for Ireland."

"Cheers!" the second guy says and they both toss back their drinks.

"Where in Ireland are you from?" the first man asks.

"Dublin," he tells him.

"I'm from Dublin, too. I can't believe it!" the first man says. "Let's have another drink to Dublin!"

"What school did you go to?" the first man asks.

"I went to St. Peter's," the second says. "I graduated in 77."

"I went to St. Peter's and graduated in 77 to. This is just unbelievable!" the first man says.

A man then walks in, sits down at the bar, looks up at the bartender ad asks him, "What's going on?"

"Not a whole lot," he says. "The O'Malley twins are drunk again."

A man comes home to find his wife with all her bags packed getting into a cab.

"Where are you going?" he asks her.

"I'm leaving you and it's because you're a pedophile!" she screams at him.

"Well," he says. "That's a pretty big word for a 9-year old."

Two lawyers are walking down the beach when they come across a naked woman in the surf. They pull her onto dry surf.

The first lawyer looks around and says, "Let's screw her."

The second lawyer shakes his head and says, "Out of what?"

A birthing coach tells all the soon-to-be mothers in his class, "All of you should know that walking while you're pregnant is very good for you. And all of you husbands, it wouldn't hurt to walk with them."

One husband asks, "Is it ok if she carries a golf bag?"

A woman has nine children over the years with her husband. When he dies, the woman is distraught, but quickly remarries.

She has seven more children only to have her second husband die on her as well.

The woman gets married for a third time and this time has six more children before she herself finally dies.

At the woman's funeral, the priest prays for her soul. "Dear God," the priest says, "Please protect the soul of this woman, who fulfilled your commandment to go forth and multiply. And we thank you Lord that they are finally together."

Leaning over to his neighbor, one of the mourners asks, "Do you think he's referring to her first or second husband?"

"I think he means her legs." the other mourner says.

The day finally arrived when Forest Gump died and went to Heaven.

He is met at the pearly gates by St. Peter himself. However, the gates are closed and Forest approaches St. Peter.

St. Peter says, "Well, Forest, it is certainly good to see you. We have heard a lot about you. I have to tell you though, the place is filling up fast and we've been administering an entrance exam for everyone. The test is short, but you have to pass it before you can get into Heaven."

Forest says, "It sure is good to be here, St. Peter sir, but nobody ever told me about any entrance exam. I sure hope the test ain't too hard. Life was a big enough challenge as it was."

St. Peter continued to say, "Yes, I know Forest, but the test is only three questions.

First, what two days of the week begin with the letter T? Second, how many seconds are there in a year? And, third, what is God's first name?"

Forest leaves to think the questions over. He returns the next day and sees St. Peter who waves him over and says, "Now that you've had a chance to think the questions over, tell me your answers."

Forest replies, "Well, the first one, which two days in the week begin with the letter "T"? Shucks, that one was easy. That would he today and tomorrow."

St. Peter's eyes open wide and he exclaims, "Forest, that is not what I was thinking, but you do have a point and I guess I did not specify so I will give you credit for that answer. How about the next one?" asked St. Peter.

"How many seconds in a year? Now that one was a little harder." Forest replied. "But I thunk about that and I guess the only answer could be twelve."

Astounded, St. Peter asks, "Twelve? Twelve? Forest, how in Heaven's name could you come up with twelve seconds in a year?"

Forest responds, "Shucks, there've got to be twelve: January 2nd, February 2nd, March 2nd, etc!"

"Hold on just a minute." St. Peter says. "I see where you are going with this and I see your point, though that was not quite what I had in mind, but I will have to give you credit for that one, too. Let's go on with the third and final question. Can you tell me God's first name?"

"Sure," Forest replied. "It's Andy."

"Andy?" exclaimed an exasperated St. Peter. "Ok, I can understand how you came up with your answers to my first two questions, but how in the world did you come up with the name Andy for the first name of God?"

"Shucks, that was the easiest one of all," Forest says. "I learnt that from the song, 'Andy walks with me, Andy talks with me, Andy tells me I am His own..."

St. Peter opened the pearly gates and said, "Run Forest, run!"

Walter Allen

IN THE _____ COURT OF THE

STATE OF _____

_____   PLAINTIFF

VS   CASE NO: XO-4301-10

_____   DEFENDANT

ARREST WARRANT

A warrant for the arrest of your heart has been issued, due to the fact that it belongs to me now. You are no longer in control of it. I must also inform you that, you have the right to remain silent while I kiss you from head to toe. You also have the right before sexual gratification to be represented by a marriage license. Anything that you say or scream during sexual gratification will be heavily weighed in your favor in the court of love.

DEFAULT JUDGEMENT

Please be advised that once signed, this warrant goes into effect immediately without further notice. Your signature is required for this legal document. No other will be issued and this court will be forced to plead a case of total unrestrained desire and satisfaction, which will result in further sexual actions against your sweet body, to include, but not limited to the following:

A) Licking and kissing you until you pass out.

B)   Blowing your mind, exotic stimulation in every imaginable way for years to come.

SENTENCING
Your sentence has already been decided for the benefit of all parties involved. You have been found GUILTY of love in the first degree. The state of MY HEART demands the maximum punishment. You are hereby sentenced to life (with me) without the possibility of parole. You will consequently be loved and cherished forever in a maximum security facility called MY HEART.

The party involved must sign below verifying that this summons was received and read.

_____   _____

X   DATE

NOTE: By signing this summons, you have been formally sentenced to LIFE WITH ME !

CC: Clerk Of Courts
       Public Defender
       Presiding Judge
       Defendant

ABOUT THE AUTHOR

All my friends call me "Bunk." I am 30 years old and from New Castle, Delaware. I am locked up for 2 counts of armed robbery. One robbery in Pennsylvania which is what I am serving time for now, and another robbery I still have to do 4 ½ -5 years in Delaware, I am hoping to start that sentence in September/October 2010.

I have been locked up now since April 2003.

I have a really good sense of humor and can be a clown at the right (and sometimes the wrong) time. I love making people laugh. I just love the fun of it and enjoy life as it comes.

I'm not a baller or shot caller; I'm just your average guy who made some mistakes, actually a couple mistakes, and I'm paying the price for those mistakes.

You can send me an email and the company (Jail-Mailman.com) will get them to me, but it's better to write directly to me at the following address or check website for current address:

Walter Allen # FZ-4301
SCI-Forest
P O Box 945
Marienville, PA 16239
waltera@Jail-Mailman.com

Walter Allen

Made in the USA
Columbia, SC
04 October 2024

43597912R00183